JOHN
FOR BEGINNERS

Also by James Taylor

Precious Days & Practical Love: *Caring for Your Aging Parent*
Everyday Psalms
Everyday Parables: *Learning from Life*
Sin: *A New Understanding of Virtue and Vice*
Letters to Stephen: *A Father's Journey of Grief and Recovery*

Christmas 2001,
To Dale Williams
From Mother and
Miriam ♡!
— Thanks!
To you and to
our Dear Lord
Jesus Christ!

JOHN
FOR BEGINNERS

A Bible Study for
Individual & Group Use

JAMES TAYLOR

WOOD LAKE BOOKS

Editor: Mike Schwartzentruber
Cover and interior design: Margaret Kyle
Cover artwork: Don Bishop, Calligraphic Backgrounds, Artville™

We acknowledge the financial support of the Government of Canada, through the Book Publishing Industry Development Program (BPIDP) for our publishing activities.

At Wood Lake Books we practice what we publish, guided by a concern for fairness, justice, and equal opportuinity in all of our relationships with employees and customers.

We recycle and reuse and encourage readers to do the same. Resources are printed on recycled paper and more environmentally friendly groundwood papers (newsprint), whenever possible. The trees used are replaced through donations to the Scoutrees for Canada program. A percentage of all profit is donated to charitable organizations.

National Library of Canada Cataloguing in Publication Data
Taylor, James, 1936-
   John for beginners
   ISBN 1-55145-496-3
   1. Bible. N.T. John – Study and teaching. 2. Bible. N.T. John – Commentaries. I. Title.
BS2616.T39 2001   226.5'07   C2001-910830-3

Copyright © 2001 James Taylor
All rights reserved. No part of this publication may be reproduced – except in the case of brief quotations embodied in critical articles and reviews – stored in an electronic retrieval system, or transmitted in any form or by any means, electronic, mechanical, photocopying, recording, or otherwise, without prior written consent of the publisher or copyright holder.

Published by Wood Lake Books Inc.
Kelowna, British Columbia, Canada
www.joinhands.com

Printing 10 9 8 7 6 5 4 3 2 1

Printed in Canada by Transcontinental Printing

CONTENTS

Introduction:
   About the Gospel of John 7

The Gospel of John:
   Commentary, Ponderings, Prayers 13

Leading a Study Group 93

Appendix 1: Lectionary Index 98

Appendix 2: Sunday Index 104

Introduction

ABOUT THE GOSPEL OF JOHN

New Testament scholar William Barclay called the Gospel of John "the most precious book in the world."

When my mother died at two o'clock one April morning, my father read through the Gospel of John before he came to waken me. That's how precious it was to him.

But John poses problems. Its chronology doesn't agree with the other three gospels. It tells different stories. It includes a number of long and complex speeches. And it includes none of Jesus' parables.

Thus, for a variety of reasons, John has fallen out of favor in some scholarly circles. This book is not about those academic arguments. Christians value the Gospel of John, not because it received scholarly approval, but because, as Barclay noted, "It is the book above all on which they feed their minds and nourish their hearts and in which they rest their souls."

The text itself, as it exists, as it has been passed down through the centuries, is what matters.

John's was almost certainly the last of the gospels to be written. That gives it a special status. There were other gospels around. "Gospel" simply means "good news." During the first century, dozens of other gospels circulated among Christians. Some of these were unknown until the discovery of the Nag Hammadi manuscripts in Egypt, a collection of writings associated with the Gnostic sect of Christianity. Some are highly fanciful. A few of these newly found writings, such as the Gospel of Thomas, are being treated as authoritative records of the life and/or teachings of Jesus. But Gnosticism was considered a heresy by the orthodox leaders of the church. And because John's gospel had some Gnostic influences, it barely made it into the "canon," the officially recognized books of the Bible.

The four historically accepted gospels, though placed at the beginning of the New Testament, did not come first chronologically. Paul's letters came first. Paul began writing what J.B. Phillips called

Letters to Young Churches roughly around 50 AD, while stories of Jesus were still being circulated orally. The first gospel written was probably Mark's, around 60 AD, followed by Matthew and Luke within the next decade.

John wrote his gospel closer to the turn of the century. Tradition attributes the gospel to the disciple John, the brother of James. The gospel itself never names the disciple John – only John the Baptist, and John the father of Simon Peter – but it does refer to "the disciple whom Jesus loved." Hence the usual assumption that John wrote about himself anonymously.

John – whether or not he was the original disciple – treats the story differently from the writers of the other gospels.

He ignores their order of events, for one thing. Matthew and Luke, having borrowed much of their material from Mark, also borrow Mark's chronology. That is, they have Jesus starting his ministry at the Jordan, then moving through Galilee, and from there into the neighboring Gentile territories. He didn't go to Jerusalem until his final week of life.

John, on the other hand, starts Jesus' ministry with a wedding celebration. He has Jesus going to Jerusalem at least three times. He locates most of his narrative in Judea, the surroundings of Jerusalem.

John also tells the story differently. When Dorothy L. Sayers – yes, the same one who pioneered murder mysteries with Lord Peter Wimsey and Hercule Poirot – wrote a series of radio plays called *The Man Born to Be King* for the British Broadcasting Corporation in the 1950s, she commented:

> Of the four Evangels, St. John's is the only one that claims to be the direct report of an eye-witness. And to any one accustomed to the imaginative handling of documents, the internal evidence bears this out. It is St. John who reports the words and actions of the individual unrepeated occasion... It is, generally speaking, John who knows the time of year, the time of day, where people sat, and how they got from one place to another. It is John who remembers not only what Jesus said, but what

the other people said to him, who can reproduce the cut-and-thrust of controversy and the development of an argument. It is John who faithfully reproduces the emphasis and repetition of a teacher trying to get a new idea across to a rather unintelligent and inattentive audience... (The Man Born to Be King, pp. 33-34.)

The other gospels focus almost exclusively on what *Jesus* said and did. They behave, in that sense, like the shrieking fans of today's rock stars. They care about what the "star" says and does; they have little interest in anyone else.

John, by contrast, tells both sides of a story. We hear not only what Jesus said and did, but how others responded and reacted to him. John gives us their words too. Dorothy Sayers offers a writer's perspective:

> When John is the authority for any scene, or when John's account is at hand to supplement those of the [other gospels] the playwright's task is easy. Either the dialogue is all there – vivid and personal on both sides – or the part of the interlocutor can be readily reconstructed from the replies given...

In that sense, John comes closer to what we know of Jesus himself as a storyteller than any of the other gospel writers.

John also tells fewer stories than the other gospels, but tells them in much greater detail, and often with long and convoluted theological explanations.

Because of these differences between John's gospel and the other three gospels, there has been a tendency during the last century to discount John's gospel. It was written too late to have been a true first person account, the critics say. It contains long speeches and explanations that don't sound like the terse aphorisms uttered by the Jesus of the other gospels. The Jesus Seminar, in fact, credits only one saying in the whole of John's gospel as possibly true to Jesus!

I evaluate John's gospel by different criteria.

First, as a storyteller myself, I find John's narrative a credible eye-witness account. If he wasn't there himself to hear the give and take between Jesus and the people he met, then he got his material directly from someone who was there. Or else he was a writer of fiction who surpassed Homer, Virgil, and the other greats of literature right up to William Shakespeare and Jane Austen. No one else – no one – handles dialogue like John for another 1500 years. That's as much of a miracle as anything recounted in the gospel itself.

Second, John must have been aware of other writings already circulating among the Christian churches. Matthew, Mark, and Luke – commonly called the synoptic gospels – were widely known. But they were certainly not the only gospels available. We've known for a long time that there must have been at least one other gospel, called "Q" (for "Quelle," meaning "source" in German), from which Matthew and Luke drew about half of their material. For a while, we assumed that was all there was. Then the discovery at Nag Hammadi, in Egypt, revealed that there may have been dozens of other "gospels" circulating, as I've already mentioned.

John cannot have been ignorant of them. So where he differs from the older gospels, I have to assume that he was, in his own way, trying to set the record straight, to clarify misunderstandings, or to remind readers of significant stories being ignored.

About the lectionary references

A lectionary is a way of organizing readings from the Bible in worship so that, over a three-year period, worshippers will hear all of the major themes and stories. Today, almost all major denominations use some form of lectionary.

The Roman Catholic Church's Second Vatican Council provided the impetus for today's use of lectionaries. They published, in 1969, a pattern based on more or less sequential reading of the synoptic gospels over a three-year period, matching the gospel passages with selections from the Epistles (letters to the early churches), Psalms, and Hebrew scriptures.

The idea caught the imagination of North American denominations. The lectionary did two things. It prevented preachers from harping continually on their own favorite passages. And in a time of decreasing loyalty to denominations, it ensured that church-hoppers would get exposed to roughly the same readings wherever they happened to worship.

Over the next years, many denominations developed their own variants of the Roman Catholic lectionary. By the 1980s, a whole diversity of lectionaries had evolved. To bring about some ecumenical coherence, a group called the Consultation on Common Texts brought out the *Common Lectionary* in 1983.

They followed that, in 1992, with the *Revised Common Lectionary*. Most mainline churches today use some form of the *Revised Common Lectionary*, although there remain some variations.

The readings shown in this commentary on the Gospel of John are taken mainly from the *Revised Common Lectionary*, though I have indicated where the readings may vary for two major groups – the Evangelical Lutheran churches (ELC) and the Roman Catholic churches (RC) of Canada and the United States. I have not, however, identified every variation in the headings. When the reading prescribed by the Lutheran or Roman Catholic lectionaries diverges by only a verse or two, I have simply included it under the reading recommended by the RCL.

For further reference, an appendix at the back of the book lists the RCL, ELC, and RC readings in more detail, sorted both according to the Gospel of John and according to the sequence of Sundays in the calendar.

About the format

I find that my comprehension of biblical texts is greatly enhanced by interaction with other people. Almost always, others have some perspectives or insights that I had not thought of. I don't have to agree with them – but in considering their understandings (or misunderstandings) I gain unexpected insights myself.

Ideally, I would hope that readers will use my comments on the Gospel of John as a launching pad for discussion with others. But that's not always possible. So, in an attempt to encourage reflection by individual readers, to force you to do more than casually accept my commentary as authoritative truth, I have included some questions, called "Ponderings." If you use them, please take some time with them. Roll them around in your mind. Let them open up new avenues of thought which might not have occurred to you otherwise.

These "Ponderings" could, of course, also be used in study groups. For more suggestions about using this book for study groups, see the section "Leading a Study Group" appendix at the back of the book.

After the "Ponderings," I have included a short prayer of one or two sentences. I've made it personal. Please treat the "I" and "me" as terms of your own. Sometimes I have addressed the prayer to God, sometimes to Jesus, and sometimes to no one in particular. The names merely reflect my mood at the time of writing. Don't feel bound by them. If you choose to use the prayer, address it to whomever you feel comfortable speaking to. Let it be a beginning, to get you started on expressing your own prayer thoughts.

John 1:1-14

All: Christmas Day, ABC
RC & ELC: Christmas 2, ABC
RC: All Souls Day, B

The timing of the gospels reveals the evolving theology of the early church.

Mark, the first gospel, didn't bother mentioning Jesus' origins. Jesus himself was enough.

Matthew and Luke each gave us quite different nativity stories – although legends might be a better description. Matthew portrays Jesus as the one who will have a kingdom; kings come to pay homage. Luke gives him divine origins, to set the stage for calling him the Son of God.

John, the last of the gospels, shifts the focus from the human to the cosmic.

Sometimes, when I take our dog for a walk at night, I look up and find myself stunned by the night sky, by thousands of universes dappling the darkness, stretching all the way to the edge of anything.

That's what John does in his prologue. He tries to stun us, shock us, into opening our minds to a much vaster view than we had held previously. This is not just about one man. Or about one nation. Or about one particular religious faith. It is not even about humans. It is about the reason and purpose of everything.

Literally everything.

In this prologue, John sets the stage for all that follows. He asserts that Jesus and God are indistinguishable.

Ponderings

- Have you ever peered through a microscope and discovered the teeming life within a single drop of water? Were you fascinated? Or repulsed?
- Where are you most likely to experience awe and wonder?
- Which idea of Jesus makes you less comfortable – Jesus as a ceramic souvenir safely stored on a shelf? Or Jesus as the force of gravity, holding planets in their paths?

Prayer

Jesus, keep me from simplifying you down to my own size. Remind me that whenever I think I have you figured out, you are always more.

John 1:10-18
All: Christmas 2, ABC

From a cosmic perspective – the widest possible lens – the writer of this gospel zooms in. But not to focus on the human individual we call Jesus; that will come later.

Rather, Jesus becomes the lens through which we see our world and our lives in a new light. The one who was indistinguishable from God came to live among us, and we humans were so preoccupied with our own navels that we missed him.

Worse, we killed him.

The little community museum near my home has a wonderful collection of butterflies. All dead. Skewered by long pins, stuck to a board.

A few people had the imagination to see the butterfly while it lived, John says. They were thrilled by its beauty and grace. It gladdened their hearts. But others skewered it, nailed it to a crossbeam.

Now, to learn about that butterfly, we have to hear the stories of those who knew it, when it was alive.

Ponderings

- Would you rather see a grizzly alive, pacing the forest, or hear about it from others?
- Do you believe what others tell you?
- What makes their stories credible?

Prayer

Jesus, have I been so busy analyzing evidence about you that I have failed to get to know you as a person?

John 1:6-8, 19-28
All: Advent 3, B

In these two groups of verses, interwoven into John's presentation of the Cosmic Christ, we learn of John the Baptist, the prophet who prepared the way for the Christ.

I wonder, sometimes, if John the Baptist saw himself just as the warm-up act for Jesus.

That's the impression that all four gospels give, of course. They go to considerable lengths to quote John the Baptist himself, stating that he accepted his role as a forerunner. He was there only to proclaim the coming of "one who is more powerful than I."

Yet the fact that all four gospels have to make this point – when only two of them felt any need to describe Jesus' birth – makes me think that John's disciples may have been a serious competitor for the early Christian church. Not all who flocked to hear John down along the Jordan later switched their allegiance to Jesus. John's movement had its own missionaries. Some of them preceded Paul into the Mediterranean. Apollos, for example, was initially a convert of John, not of Jesus (Acts 18:25). John had followers in Ephesus before Paul got there (Acts 19:1–4). Some historical records suggest that John's "church" thrived for several centuries. But they never totally died out. The Mandaeans in Iraq today still claim to be the direct spiritual descendants of John the Baptist.

That expansion wasn't John's doing. He had been beheaded long before. But his followers were not content to let his message die with him.

Perhaps those disciples of John the Baptist misunderstood his mission. They were not willing to see him merely as a forerunner for someone else. If they were competition for Jesus' followers, the only argument that could really dissuade them would be their founder's own words.

Ponderings
- How did you recently misunderstand someone else's intentions?
- Did you defend yourself? Did you try to prove you were right, after all?
- If John the Baptist's followers misunderstood his intentions, is it possible Christians might also have misunderstood Jesus' intentions?

Prayer
I am sometimes too easily swayed by personality and charisma. I need the insight to sift through competing claims for my loyalty.

John 1:29-42
All: Epiphany 2, A

In this story, John's gospel puts a different spin on two accounts in the synoptic gospels.

First, at Jesus' baptism, the other gospels describe the voice from heaven either as something seen and heard by all (Matthew and Luke), or as a private experience of Jesus himself (Mark). This version makes John the Baptist the source of information.

Second, it asserts that at least a few of Jesus' disciples were initially disciples of John the Baptist. The synoptic gospels (see Matthew 4:18-23, for example) state that Jesus called Simon and Andrew, and James and John, directly from their fishing livelihood, without any warning. But John's version says that Andrew, and maybe others, hung out with John the Baptist first.

Both versions may be correct. But John's narrative suggests, at the very least, that Andrew and Simon, later known as Peter, were more than simple fishing folk. They were already discontent with the status quo. They had been exposed to John the Baptist's passionate rhetoric. They were looking for something. Or someone.

If Jesus saw them with John the Baptist and then recognized them again at the lake, he may have sensed that they would be receptive.

So when Jesus called them at the lakeshore, as the story is told in the synoptics, they were ready to drop everything and go.

Ponderings
- What persons matter enough to you that if they called, you would drop everything and respond immediately?
- Do you think you have ever heard Jesus call you? What did you do about it?
- Are you carrying too much stuff from the past around with you to respond quickly?

Prayer
I would like to be ready when you call, Lord. Help me keep my ears clean, my mind open, and my baggage light.

John 1:43–51
All: Epiphany 2, B
ELC: St. Bartholomew, ABC

Pop artist Andy Warhol said that in the television age, each of us gets 15 minutes of fame. This story is Nathanael's 15 minutes. He never shows up again, but for a few glorious moments, all the floodlights of history focus on him.

And he utters a racist comment. "Can anything good come out of Nazareth?" he asks scornfully. Archie Bunker would have been proud of him.

Though not stated as explicitly, the theme shows up repeatedly through the Gospel of John. Over and over, skeptics insist that Jesus cannot be the promised Messiah, because "we know where he comes from."

Philip, the other character in this scene, appears several more times. "Come and see," he says. It too becomes a recurring theme. "Show us the Father, and we will believe," he says to Jesus, in John 14. And in Acts 8, after converting a Samaritan magician, he meets an Ethiopian eunuch and offers to guide him through the scriptures, so that he can understand what he's reading.

Rather than telling us what to believe, John prefers to tell stories. Like Jesus telling parables, he expects us to deduce the story's significance. As a writer, I ask, "Why tell this story; at this point? How does it advance the plot?"

Aside from introducing Philip, this scene probably centers on Nathanael's astonished insight: "Rabbi, you are the son of God!" It sets the stage for the drama that follows, the curtain raiser for the scenes to come. The other three gospels have Peter making this discovery, midway through Jesus' ministry. John wants it to come at the very beginning, so that his readers can't miss the point of the rest of his stories.

Ponderings
- Do you ever have unexpected insights? Perhaps into how relationships work, or social systems, or…
- Do you tend to judge people by their origins? By where they come from, or who their parents were?

- Would 15 minutes of fame be enough for you?

Prayer
Give me important insights, God. But even more, help me to recognize them when I have them, and to remember them.

John 2:1-11
All: Epiphany 2, C

According to John, Jesus' first miracle – the first evidence of his nature as Messiah – was turning water into wine at a wedding feast.

John Spong has suggested this may have been Jesus' own wedding banquet. It's the only way, he argues, that Jesus or his mother could order servants around.

Others suggest that Jesus fouled up the wedding arrangements by showing up with a handful of thirsty new fishing friends. They drank more than the host expected. So supplies ran out – and Jesus, as the cause of this shortfall, was expected to remedy it.

People with a more spiritual bent interpret the story symbolically. They see this wedding feast – like the parables of wedding banquets (Matthew 22:1-14, Luke 14:15-24) – as a foretaste of the promised "Kingdom of God."

I prefer a parallel to the Parable of the Sower (Matthew 13:1-9, Mark 4:1-9, Luke 8:4-8). Although a smart farmer would plant seed only where it had the best chance of growing to maturity, this "sower" scatters seed indiscriminately. The sower distributes seeds, in fact, the way God does. Plants disperse seeds in birds' bellies, on the wind, on animals' fur, in streams. Salmon fertilize an entire stream where only a few eggs will mature and return to start the cycle again.

The Sower is a parable, not of prudence, but of wasteful generosity.

So is the story of the wedding at Cana. Where human provision fails, God provides abundantly – about 150 gallons of wine, more than the guests can drink, and certainly more than they deserve.

Whether this story is fact or fabrication, it conveys the profligate generosity, the unconditional gifts, of God.

Jesus' response to his mother may seem harsh: "What's it to you, woman?" But for John the storyteller, it serves to introduce yet another recurring theme. "My time has not yet come," Jesus continues. For the first readers of this gospel, the wonder of Jesus' resurrection surrounded everything they read, like a frame around a picture. They would recognize this "time" as the moment of revelation when Jesus was recognized as the personification of God.

The whole Gospel of John focuses forward to that moment of Jesus' glory.

Ponderings
- Do you suppose the wedding guests remembered to say "Thank you" for their host's generosity?
- What unexpected gift have you received recently?
- Do you always remember to be grateful for God's generosity?

Prayer
Thank you, God. I am grateful. A small ray of joy can brighten the gloomiest of days.

John 2:13-22
All: Lent 3, B
RC: St. John Lateran

Again, John changes the chronology of the other gospels. They all put the confrontation in the temple at the end of Jesus' ministry, as the culminating affront that pushed the religious authorities over the edge. They could no longer tolerate this Galilean rabble-rouser. So they had to find a way of getting rid of him.

John puts the story at the beginning. Again, I ask why? It could be, of course, as some have argued, that Jesus trashed the temple more than once. But that assumes that John is trying to write history. He's not – he's stringing together stories, one after the other, to make a point.

I suggest that the reason for telling this story, here, comes in verse 22: "After he was raised...his disciples remembered..."

All of these stories, John tells us, were just ordinary events when they happened. They only took on significance later.

Our son died of cystic fibrosis at 21. Before he died, I got frustrated with him. Each year at camp, he tackled something new. One year, he earned his master canoeist's certificate. Another year, it was water skiing. Another, sailing. "Why don't you stick with something, now you're good at it?" I demanded.

It wasn't until after he died that I understood why. He accepted, even though I didn't, that he had a limited life expectancy. He didn't want to waste any of his precious time repeating experiences unnecessarily.

But that understanding came too late for me to share with him. Just as, John tells us, it came too late for the disciples.

Ponderings
- Do things often seem clearer in hindsight?
- What prevents you from seeing things just as clearly in the present?
- What have you done that irrevocably changed the course of your life? At the time, did it seem that important?

Prayer
Sometimes I get so preoccupied with my own concerns, that I see everything through a fog of preconceptions. Give me the compassion to see more clearly.

John 3:1-17
RCL & ELC: Trinity, B
RCL & ELC: Lent 2 (alternate), A
(Also 3:16-18 RC: Trinity, B, and 3:13-17 Holy Cross, ABC)

This reading is loaded with significant verses. It could be fun to focus on individual verses, and perhaps even individual words, and study them.

But the scene as a whole demands attention. Two men meet, secretly, under cover of darkness. Nicodemus is curious, but not yet willing to risk public identification with this strange new figure on the social landscape. Nicodemus is like many today, who profess belief in God but don't want to be identified with the church. They read books on care of the soul. They study Buddhist concepts or explore astronomy to stimulate their spirituality. But they prefer to keep their faith out of the public eye.

Nicodemus is a modern person. He asks about facts, about logic, about known reality. "Can one return to the womb?" he demands, quite reasonably.

We can hear the frustration in Jesus' voice (verses 11-12). "You want to know about heaven," Jesus grumbles. "But you won't believe me when I tell you about things here on earth that you should be able to see for yourself!"

If we cannot see ourselves in Nicodemus's guarded caution, his scientific skepticism, we miss the point of this encounter.

In this dialogue Jesus describes, almost like a riddle, the mystery and implications of being born again through the Spirit. It's a pattern of dialogue that John uses repeatedly. Someone asks a question. Jesus replies with images that go right over the person's head. The rest of the passage tries to sort out the misunderstanding.

Let's ignore the scientific side of what it means to be "born again." That was what Nicodemus got hung up on. He thought it meant literally returning to the waters of the womb. He couldn't imagine any other kind of birth – or rebirth. We've pretty much gotten over that practical question, since the evangelical churches have made "born again" their battle cry.

But many Christians still leap to the conclusion that their rebirth makes them an only child. Most people think of their faith as a private relationship to God, the heavenly "Father" (who somehow has a spiritual womb). They actually resent being told that their faith has worldly implications.

The cult of individualism runs rampant through our culture. Nowhere is it more evident than in our faith.

In fact, being "born of the Spirit" implies that everyone else reborn into the family of the Spirit is a brother or sister. We therefore owe them the same obligations as we would our blood family.

Far from narrowing our horizons to God 'n' me, "born again" should broaden those horizons to include the whole household of God.

Ponderings

- What makes a person a Christian, anyway? Does it depend on having an experience, affirming a statement of faith, following an example, or behaving in a certain way?
- Do you feel closer to God when you're alone, or when you're with others?
- How many fresh starts have you had in your life? How has each one affected your relationships?

Prayer

I probably can't care as much about someone I've never met as about my closest friends and my family. But please, God, help me try.

John 3:14-21
All: Lent 4, B

This reading picks up the final verses of the previous section. In reading this passage, we need to remember that early manuscripts had no capital letters, no punctuation marks, and no sentence or paragraph breaks. The punctuation in modern Bibles is guesswork, nothing more. So we have no way of knowing exactly where Jesus' words end, and John's interpretation begins. The words attributed directly to Jesus might end after verse 15, or verse 16. That would make the judgmental sentiments of verses 17-21 part of John's editorial commentary, rather than Jesus' direct teaching.

The later verses also pick up one of John's favorite analogies, of Jesus as light. But verses 14-15 start with Jesus comparing himself to a snake.

In Numbers (21:4-9) the Israelites were complaining – again – about having been taken from the fleshpots of Egypt into the wilderness. To punish them, God sent a plague of poisonous snakes. When Moses interceded on their behalf – again – God told him to fasten a bronze snake to a pole and hold it aloft like a banner. As long as the people focused their eyes (and their attention) on this rallying point, they were protected against the venomous snakes.

The snake, therefore, gave them the gift of life. That's why a snake wrapped around a staff is still the symbol for physicians around the world.

But we don't normally associate snakes with healing. When we think snake, we think evil.

Our attitude is dominated by a single story – the Garden of Eden legend. Other cultures are more likely to venerate snakes. The ruins of Chichén Itzá in Mexico, for example, display rattlesnake icons everywhere. The snake's ability to shed its skin made it, for the Maya, a symbol of resurrection.

Because of Eden, though, we usually identify the serpent with Satan.

But Jesus isn't blinded by that one portrayal. As usual, in creating a figure of speech, he links together two dissimilar things to light up our imaginations. If people gave him the same undivided attention that they had given Moses' bronze snake in the desert, he said, they too could be healed. They could receive God's pardon. They would receive life. And more than life. They would receive eternal life.

I've taken longer than usual on this metaphor, because it illustrates both Jesus' process, and the difficulties we have with it. We stumble over some of Jesus' parables because we no longer think the way he did. Like Nicodemus, we tend to think and speak factually and literally. We expect his poetic figures of speech to be as clearly defined as a mathematical formula or an engineering experiment. We have lost the skill of thinking metaphorically.

When Jesus created his parables, he picked only one quality, the one that made the point he wanted to make. So he didn't say, speaking of mustard seeds, that the Kingdom could burn your mouth or taste good on a hot dog. He didn't suggest, referring to lost coins, that the Kingdom might be covered with dustballs. Matthew tells us, "He did not say anything to them without using a parable" (13:34). Unless we're prepared to miss Jesus' point – or worse, to ignore it because we can't make rational sense of it – we have to learn to think as he did, metaphorically.

Ponderings
- Did figures of speech bore you in high school English literature classes?
- Are you aware of the figures of speech you use yourself?
- Is a figure of speech true? Or false? Or neither? Or both?

Prayer
I can analyze Jesus' parabolic sayings into dusty death. Or I can simply let them speak to me. Which will I choose?

John 3:22-31
Not in lectionary
Once again, the gospel needs to bring back John the Baptist to assure readers that Jesus, not John, was the long promised Messiah.

John 4:5-42
All: Lent 3 A
Like the John 3:14-21 reading, many sermons could be preached on isolated verses.
- The woman, and her record of relationships with men.
- The fact that Jesus talked – let alone discussed theology – with a woman, and worse, with a Samaritan.
- His references to living water, especially in the context of the water gushing from the rock in the desert.
- His claim that the "fields are ripe for the harvest."
- The woman's restoration to credibility in village life…

But as with Nicodemus, the real story lies in the interaction between the two. Because there shouldn't have been any. By law and by custom, Jesus should not have talked with a woman at all. And doubly not with a Samaritan. And particularly not about theological matters. And least of all should he have drunk from her cup. She was unclean!

For a comparable situation, imagine not just sitting and talking with one of today's outcasts – such as a person dying of AIDS – but sharing his cup, his toothbrush, even his needles. That's how unthinkable Jesus' actions were to people of his time.

But a historical perspective makes this passage even more offensive to devout Jews. For in this interaction, Jesus plays the part of the stiff-necked and ungrateful Hebrews at Massah and Meribah, demanding water where no water should be available (Exodus 17:2-7). And she – the woman, the Samaritan – plays the roles of God and Moses, bringing forth water from the rock where a well had been dug by their common ancestor Jacob.

Out of that interaction, the woman is changed. She has been treated not just as a person, but as an equal. When the conversation gets uncomfortable, she diverts it into theological abstractions. And Jesus takes her seriously.

By the time the conversation is over, she no longer skulks to the well in the heat of the day, avoiding the other women of the village. She runs back, openly, inviting disbelief and incredulity. The other villagers set aside their suspicions, and see for themselves, and are convinced.

John's juxtaposition of stories drives the point home. Nicodemus, an aristocratic Jew, doesn't believe. The Samaritan villagers, who occupied a position on the Jewish social totem pole slightly below ground level, do believe. According to John's gospel, they are the first to accept Jesus as Christ.

John's gospel tends to take a harsher attitude toward "the Jews" than the other gospels. A great deal of the gospel deals with the increasingly bitter confrontation between Jesus and the Jewish authorities. I suspect that John deliberately put these two stories back to back, to emphasize the rejection of Jesus by his own religious leaders.

Ponderings

- What group or class of people would you feel most uncomfortable associating with? Why?
- Is there anyone you avoid having a conversation with? Is there anyone who avoids having a conversation with you?
- Do you ever say something just to see what kind of reaction it will provoke? Could John have been doing that here?

Prayer

God, forgive me for sometimes treating people as hopeless cases who will never ever see the light.

John 4:46-54
Not in lectionary

If John wasn't an eyewitness to the events he describes, then he was the first modern fiction writer. Listen to the detail in this story, the first of a series about healing. Jesus has returned to Cana where, according to John's chronology, he began his ministry. An official from Capernaum, a town at least a day's walk away, comes to see him. Assured that his son will live, the official starts to return home.

His slaves come rushing to meet him halfway home, to say that the boy is okay, after all.

Just in case anyone should express skepticism – "Aw, the kid might have been getting better anyway" – John specifies the exact time when the boy began to recover.

Now John's hearers have a choice. Either Jesus healed a dying boy at long distance. Or, somehow, also at long distance, he knew exactly when a boy naturally took a turn for the better.

If you don't want to believe one miracle, says John, you will have to believe the other.

Ponderings

- Define "miracle" in your own words.
- Have you ever experienced a miracle yourself?
- If miracles can be explained, does that make them any less of a miracle for the persons involved?

Prayer

Skepticism is an easy way to distance myself from situations I have difficulty understanding. May I have the insight and empathy to see those situations from the perspective of those directly involved in them.

John 5:1-9 (10-18)
RCL & ELC: Easter 6, C (alternate)

The healings continue. To ensure no one still thinks the last healing might be just coincidence, John adds a telling detail – this victim had been ill for 38 years. He was not just pretending, and he had not suffered a short-term malfunction.

The dialogue confirms the detail. The pool bubbled periodically, like a less-vigorous version of Old Faithful. Only those who got into the water during the bubbling got healed. But this man was too sick to lead the rush. Others pushed past him.

And he had no family to tip him in.

Jesus follows John's familiar pattern in his relationship with the sick man. He opens the conversation; then he throws a curve ball. Usually, it's a cryptic statement, misunderstood by his partner in conversation. This time, his words are not cryptic, but are still a challenge: "Do you want to be healed? Do you *really* want to be healed?"

It was a valid question. After 38 years, the man was growing elderly. He had no skill, no profession. Once healed, he would have to start a new life. Jesus told Nicodemus of the need to be "born anew" spiritually; this man would have to be "born anew" in real life.

"Yes," the man said. And that willingness was all that he needed to get started on a new life.

Verses 10-18, though not in the lectionary, continue the story. The temple authorities accuse the healed man of breaking the laws against doing work on the Sabbath. Like Adam in Eden, the man tries to divert the criticism to someone else. "Don't blame me," he defends himself. "This guy made me do it."

After Jesus renews contact with the man in the temple, the man snitches on him. The authorities transfer their attacks to Jesus. In his defense, Jesus makes a radical claim – if God doesn't stop working on the Sabbath, neither need he.

Ponderings
- Would you like to start your life again?
- What would you change? What would you do the same again?
- Do you attribute healing powers to moving water? Do you use a hot tub? A whirlpool bath? Ever sat under a waterfall?

Prayer

I know that some parts of me need healing. But I'm afraid to jump in the deep end of the pool, in case I can't swim. Give me courage to embrace new life.

John 5:19-46
Not in lectionary

In the rest of this chapter, John introduces two recurring themes.
1. The people John simply labels as "the Jews" cross-examine anyone Jesus helps. Of course, all the people there were Jews. John intends to identify only the religious bigots of Judaism. Unfortunately, his choice of words contributed to centuries of anti-Semitism, as the religious bigots of Christianity took his charge literally, and sought vengeance against all Jews.
2. Jesus provides long, detailed, theological explanations for his behavior. The explanations probably came from John, or other leaders of the early church, not from Jesus. But that distinction matters only to a people (like us) who take things literally. This was what the early church believed – this was what the first readers wanted to know, not whether the words were historically accurate.

We may consider it unethical for John to put words into Jesus' mouth. After 70 years of recalling and reflecting on Jesus' words, John may no longer have known the difference between what Jesus said and what he had come to think about what Jesus said. In some ways, we understood our son Stephen better after his death than before. After 70 years, John's perceptions of Jesus, and Jesus himself, had become about as indistinguishable as Jesus and God.

Verses 19-29 begin to develop the underlying theme of John's gospel: Jesus and God are a single extended unity.

Verses 30-38 continue to assert Jesus' supremacy over John the Baptist. Only this time, instead of the affirmation coming from John, it comes from Jesus.

Verses 39-47 seem to be addressed to a different audience, those who study their scriptures and think that they have found there all the answers that they will ever need. Those persons today who treat the Bible as infallible, inerrant, and absolutely authoritative in every circumstance apparently don't read this section very often. Don't put your trust any written text, Jesus warns; trust me.

Jesus' answer to criticism, in summary, goes something like this.
- Believe me.
- If you won't believe me, believe John the Baptist.
- If you won't believe John, believe God.
- If you won't believe God, believe your own scriptures.
- If you won't believe any of those, why would you believe me?

Ponderings
- Which of your relationships are founded on trust? Are any based on distrust? Consider some examples: your mother, your teenage child, an insurance broker, a police officer, a teacher…
- Would you buy a used car from someone you didn't trust as a person?
- Can rules and regulations make someone trustworthy?

Prayer
God, I trust you. If you were embodied in a human person, I could trust that person implicitly, too. Help me make trust an operating principle in my life.

John 6:1–21
All: Proper 12, Ordinary 17, B

In this familiar story, Jesus feeds 5,000 people from five loaves and two fishes. Awed by the miracle, the people want to make him their leader, their figurehead.

Few stories, other than the crucifixion, appear in all four gospels. This is one of them, so it must have had a profound impact. But where the other three gospels simply report it, more or less objectively, John characteristically carries on to develop the theology of the event.

The primary story is, of course, the feeding of the 5,000. John does not include the Last Supper in the Upper Room; for him, this story becomes his justification for the institution of the Eucharist. Jesus gave thanks (*eucharistia* in Greek). John does not say, though the parallels in all three synoptic gospels do (Matthew 14, Mark 6, Luke 9), that he blessed and broke the bread – the characteristic gesture that enabled two disciples to recognize him after his resurrection (Luke 24:30–31).

The people's affirmation of Jesus as prophet is not merely because they have full bellies. Feeding people miraculously was a prophetic tradition: Moses in the desert (Exodus 16); Elijah with the widow of Zarephath (1 Kings 17:8–16); Elisha with 100 men (2 Kings 4:42–44).

Matthew, Mark, and John all follow this story with Jesus walking on the water. Presumably, they want to identify Jesus' supernatural powers beyond any challenge. Perhaps even back then, skeptics tried to explain away the miracle of the feeding: "Well, yes, but what he really did was encourage everyone by his example to get out their own lunches and share them." By adding the story of Jesus walking on water, the gospel writers retort: "Then explain this one away!"

Ponderings

- Do you seek scientific explanations for baffling events? Would you like to know exactly how Jesus walked on water, or fed the 5,000? If you got such an explanation, how would it change your concept of Jesus?
- How do you feel about politicians who try to buy your votes with handouts?
- In the wilderness, Jesus rejected the temptation to attract followers by feeding them. Did he violate his own principles with the 5,000?

Prayer

Jesus, you taught your disciples to pray, "Do not put us to the test." Forgive us, please, for constantly putting everything you said and did to the test.

John 6:24-35
All: Proper 13, Ordinary 18, B
RCL and ELC: Thanksgiving C

Unlike the other gospel writers, John is not content merely to tell the story of feeding the 5,000. He makes sure no one misses the point, by linking this feeding to the Exodus story of Moses providing manna for the Hebrew people in the desert. The connection implies that what Moses was to the Jewish people, Jesus is to the new Christian church.

In the temptations in the wilderness, Jesus refused to win followers by feeding them. The feeding of the 5,000 proved the wisdom of his decision. The people followed him across the lake. But Jesus knew what they wanted – food, shelter, security. He knew he offered them the opposite – a life of risk, suffering, and vulnerability.

"You are looking for me," he told them bluntly, "because you ate your fill."

Their minds were still running on food. They compare him to Moses, who gave the people manna in the desert.

"You got it wrong again," Jesus told them (paraphrased, of course). "Give the credit where it belongs – to God. Not to me or to Moses."

The people had a "Messiah complex." We might well call it a "fairy godmother" complex. They wanted some individual to solve their problems for them. All that person had to do was perform miracles.

Lots of people still have a Messiah complex. They want someone to fight their battles for them, do their thinking for them, and look after them. Political parties make messiahs of their leaders. During the 20th century, business and government treated various economists as messiahs, and followed their teachings without question, even when it imposed huge hardships on citizens and workers.

"When did you come here?" the people ask. They're still thinking of physical facts. The last time they saw him, Jesus was on the other side of the lake. They knew only one boat had left the previous evening, and he wasn't in it.

And Jesus responds crankily: "Go away. You only like me because I give you food."

The people also seem rather obtuse. "What sign will you give us?" they demand, in spite of just having had five small loaves turned into enough food for 5,000.

They think with their stomachs. They know exactly what sign they want. Moses fed his people in the desert; if Jesus is a comparable prophet, he will continue to feed them.

John sets the people up as "straight man" so that Jesus can deliver the punch lines. Their inane questions let him make his points:
- Faith in God matters more than worldly comfort.
- Jesus is the human revelation of God.
- They should not put their faith in mere humans.
- Only Jesus himself is worthy of worship.

The thread of hunger – and thirst – runs strongly all through John's gospel. In the synoptic gospels, Jesus heals; in John, he feeds. Not with bagels or burgers, but with wisdom. With himself. "I am the bread of life," he tells the crowds.

In this expansion of the story, John, more than the other three gospels, identifies Jesus with God. Not identical with God, not God masquerading as a human. That's a subtle but significant distinction. Jesus is not omnipotent, omniscient, or omnipresent. He has to walk from place to place; he gets tired; he weeps; he dies. God does not, as far as we know, suffer any of those human limitations. But in his character, his response to situations, his insights, says John, if you know Jesus, you know God.

Ponderings
- Who is your current "messiah"?
- How would you recognize a "sign" if it happened to you?
- What kind of evidence do you accept as valid? Does it have to support your preconceptions? Have you already decided what "signs" you will believe?

Prayer
When life feels empty, when I'm hungry and thirsty for meaning and purpose, please, don't let anyone feed me platitudes.

John 6:35, 41–51
All: Proper 14, Ordinary 19, B

For devout Jews, the equation of Jesus with God was blasphemy. But far from back-pedaling, Jesus plunges on. By identifying himself as "the bread of life," Jesus does something radical.

Jesus' "I AM" assertions are unique to John's gospel. In our linguistic culture, at least half of our sentences use that insignificant little verb "to be." To us, the metaphor may be startling, but not the sentence formation.

But the Aramaic language of Jesus' time didn't have a verb "to be" at all. (That verb came to us from Greek.) They expressed figures of speech by the juxtaposition of images.

The writer of John builds these images into each successive story. With Nicodemus (John 3), Jesus talks about a new birth beyond ordinary birth. With the woman at the well (John 4), Jesus talks about water that is more than water. Here, he speaks of bread that is more than bread. It is spiritual nourishment.

And, Jesus asserts, adding a further level of personification, he is that bread.

Little wonder that literal-minded listeners had difficulty understanding him!

But aside from the metaphor, when he said "I AM..." he used the name of God, the Holy One of Israel, the one whose name must not be uttered. "I am who I am," God told Moses (Exodus 3).

Thanks to the Greeks, who invented the verb "to be" and with it the whole structure of Aristotelian logic, we cannot imagine any other way of making an assertion. But to the loyal Jews of Jesus' time, even the formulation of his claim must have seemed scandalous.

Ponderings
- What kinds of statements would you consider blasphemous, beyond the limits of acceptable speech?
- What would statements that instinctively get your back up be most likely to deal with? Religion? Sexuality? Economics? Politics?
- How could you set your automatic reactions aside, to hear what the person might really be saying?

Prayer

Take the scales from my eyes, so that I may see others as they really are. In the process, let me see myself as I really am.

John 6:51–58
All: Proper 15, Ordinary 20, B
RC: Corpus Christi, A

When he calls himself "the bread of life," Jesus seems to anticipate the church's sacrament of Communion. Certainly, his words were appropriated for that ritual.

Having called himself the "bread of life," Jesus pushes his metaphor even further. It's not just that we have a hunger for something more than physical food. It's not just that we have a spiritual hunger. It's not even that our spiritual hunger can be satisfied by knowing Jesus, the bread made flesh.

No – we have to eat that flesh, absorb it, ingest it, make it an intrinsic part of ourselves, as we would eat bread.

It's not as far-fetched a concept as we, coddled in our industrial and technological cocoon, might assume. All over the world, societies that live closer to nature try to gain some of the courage of a lion by eating its heart. Even in urban societies, many men still believe that by eating an aphrodisiac made from glands of a rhino or bear, they can borrow some of its sexual prowess.

But here, I think, the historic interpretation of the church has gotten the message wrong. The doctrine of "transubstantiation" asserts that in the Eucharist, Holy Communion, the bread and wine served to the people literally become the body and blood of Jesus.

When everything else in this multi-leveled metaphor is figurative, though, I can't accept that the word "eat" must be taken literally. Jesus is not talking about cannibalism. I don't think he's even talking about eating a meal, real or sacramental. I think he's saying that his flesh must become ours, and our flesh must become his. To the watching world, he and his followers must be indistinguishable.

So it's not that bread and wine must become his flesh and blood. Rather, we must become his flesh and blood. That's the only way the world today can recognize him.

John repeats and reinforces this message more explicitly in later chapters. It's a running theme in chapters 14-17, especially 17:22-23 – "so that they may be one, as we are one, I in them and you in me, so that they may be completely one…" And it comes through in John's epilogue on the shores of Galilee (21:15-17).

This is not easy stuff. Especially for those who like simple answers.

Ponderings
- How have you traditionally explained the religious ritual called Communion, Eucharist, Mass, or the Lord's Supper?
- What does it mean to eat the body and blood of Christ?
- Does the concept of becoming the "body of Christ" frighten you?

Prayer
Take my life and let it be consecrated, Lord, to thee.

John 6:56-69
All: Proper 16, Ordinary 21, B

Jesus' multi-leveled discourse about the bread of life obviously went right over many heads. "This is tough stuff," they said (verse 60). "We just don't get it."

Many who had been following him around gave up. They voted with their feet, and left to pursue less challenging prophets.

Their kin are still around today. People don't necessarily want to know difficult truths about the economy, the environment, their relationships… Instead, they flock to those who offer them simple solutions, black and white answers to complex questions. They espouse single issues: abortion, euthanasia, gun control, free trade, interest rates, seal hunts…There are no grays, no in-betweens. Everything is absolute.

Jesus is more than most people are prepared to struggle with.

At the end of this reading, we have John's version of Peter's Great Confession. The three synoptic gospels have Peter boldly affirming, "You are the Christ!" John is more realistic, given the complexity of Jesus' teachings. "Where can we go," Peter says, helplessly. "We have come to believe that you are the Holy One of God."

Unsaid, but implied, is a footnote – "even if we have no clue what you're talking about yet."

But his disciples didn't quit. They hung in with him. In the end, perhaps that's all that matters.

Ponderings
- Do you like clear explanations?
- Do you need to understand all the implications of a proposition before you can commit yourself to it?
- If we knew all that lay ahead, would any of us ever get married or have children?

Prayer
God, you want me to set out on a journey of faith without knowing the route or the destination, at least give me confidence in my guide.

John 7:1–32
Not in lectionary

I suspect this passage was left out of the lectionary because it directly contradicts the three synoptic gospels. According to them, Jesus went to Jerusalem only once, at the end of his ministry. That visit led to his arrest, trial, and crucifixion. But John has Jesus in Jerusalem at least three times. The first time, he cleared the temple of moneychangers (2:13–25). The second time, he heals the invalid by the pool (5:1–18). Chapter 6 puts him back in Galilee; chapter 7 has him in Jerusalem again for the Festival of Booths. Chapter 10 finds him in Jerusalem once more, but this time in winter.

Some scholars suggest that the chapters have gotten out of order. That would be impossible on a scroll, but by the time this gospel was written, scrolls were reserved for sacred writings. These gospels were not considered sacred – yet. They were simply stories to inform the faithful and persuade the curious. So John wrote his text on individual sheets of paper or parchment. But the convention of page numbering – like capitals and punctuation – still had to be invented. So it's quite possible that, as the original text of the gospel got passed around, some pages got out of order. Chapter

6, based in Galilee, could possibly have been misplaced. It might belong between chapters 4 and 5.

But that's guesswork. And what we have to work with is the text, as it has come down to us. We cannot move pieces around to suit our whims.

A more serious problem is that, according to the text, Jesus tells a lie. He tells his brothers he is not going up to Jerusalem. (Several translations insert the word "yet" to make the deception less offensive.) This is not, he says, the right time – a recurring theme in this gospel.

But then, in fact, he does go. Which presents many modern Christians with a pair of equally unacceptable options. Either Jesus lied, planning to go later, in secret. Or he changed his mind. Both options contradict common assumptions about Jesus:

a) God doesn't lie. If Jesus was God, he wouldn't lie either.
b) God already knows everything. If Jesus was God, he would know everything too. There's an implicit assumption that one changes one's mind only when presented with new, previously unknown, information.

This kind of reasoning reveals that we may be thinking of Jesus as divine, and be ignoring his humanity. If he was truly human, he learned. He adapted. And he could change his mind.

The text reads much better going from verse 14 directly to verse 25. Jesus shows up in the temple, teaching; the people are amazed, because they know that his life is in danger.

Verses 15–24 probably belong in chapter 6, where Jesus was teaching the people about Moses. They wonder at his knowledge. And he goes on teaching. Quite likely, a single sheet with ten verses on it got misplaced, and ended up here.

However it happened, the verses are here now, and here we have to deal with them. The crux of the passage lies in his discussion about the Sabbath, and the law. Under the law, work of any kind was forbidden on the Sabbath. But circumcision, Jesus argues, was permitted so that the person could become a Jew and thus be enabled to obey the law.

So it's acceptable to break the law, to support the law.

In our time, it's against the law to shoot another person. But it is acceptable to shoot a crazed gunman to prevent him from shooting other people.

In a less violent mode, we all know it's not right for a stranger to grab a small child. But it is all right, if grabbing that child saves her from running in front of a passing car.

The message is clear. Laws are not absolute. They have to be considered in context.

The story continues in the temple, after the interruption of verses 15-24. The people could not accept Jesus as Messiah because they knew where he came from. Like Nathanael (1:46) they did not believe that anything good could come out of a place like Nazareth. They knew his family. There was no mystery about his origins. And that contradicted their preconceptions. They expected their Messiah to appear – Poof! – like a fairy godmother.

But a few believed him, even though others wanted to arrest him for sacrilege.

Ponderings
- Can you imagine any circumstances in which you would kill? Steal? Lie?
- Are there any absolutely unbreakable rules for living? If so, what are they?
- How do you react when someone challenges your favorite assumptions?

Prayer
God, prevent me from painting myself into corners where I have no alternative but to support extreme positions.

John 7:37-39
RCL: Pentecost (alternate), A
RC & ELC: Pentecost Vigil, A

This passage is read at Pentecost because of the connection in verse 39. It makes an interesting equation – the coming of the Holy Spirit equals the glorification of Jesus.

The larger context of this passage has Jesus talking about his eventual departure: "I will be with you a little while longer, and then I am going to him who sent me" (John 7:33). As usual, many misunderstood him. They wondered if he planned to take his message to the Jews of the Diaspora, the "lost ten tribes" who had never returned after the Exile. With the wisdom of hindsight, Jesus' followers came to realize that he was speaking about his death.

Surprisingly, John fails to dramatize Jesus' proclamation in the temple (verses 37–38). Each day of the festival, a procession of shouting, singing, palm-waving worshippers brought water to pour on the altar, in thanksgiving to God who sent rains and produced harvests. On the final day, they marched not once but seven times around the altar. And in the middle of that celebration, Jesus' voice rang out: "Let anyone who is thirsty come to me…"

Perhaps John took the context for granted.

John threads metaphors through his gospel – of bread, of light, of living water… But I wonder, sometimes, if he recognized some ironies he created. In this passage, Jesus invites those who are thirsty to come to him (7:37). He calls himself the living water: "Those who drink of the water that I give them will never be thirsty" (4:14). Yet on the cross, he himself cries out, "I am thirsty" (19:28). For water? Or for support? Was Jesus having a crisis of faith? Does his cry invalidate previous claims?

Or was John, in verse 38, foreshadowing another piece of the crucifixion story? When soldiers pierced Jesus' side with a spear, a stream of blood and water flowed from his chest.

In focusing only on Jesus' words, this abbreviated passage also ignores the effects of those words (verses 40–53). Instead of asking what Jesus meant, his hearers started arguing about his authority to say them, haggling once more about details of his genealogy and birth.

Ponderings
- Have you ever been misunderstood? Why?
- Where does the authority to speak come from? Does it derive from a person's experience? From his or her connections? From some external source?
- What are you thirsting for?

Prayer

I get bogged down in details too often. It's so easy for irrelevant trivia to get in the way of true understanding.

John 8:1-11
RC: Lent 5, C

Here's another passage that doesn't seem to belong. Some of the oldest manuscripts of John's gospel don't include the story of the woman caught in adultery at all. Some modern Bibles also omit it, or attach it as an appendix elsewhere. Other Bibles mark it as of doubtful origin.

I find it – along with the parable of the Prodigal Son and the Good Samaritan – central to my understanding of Jesus' message and personality.

Towards the end of his life, my father wrote something resembling memoirs for his granddaughter, my daughter. We found the manuscript after he died. We also found some draft pages that gave some significant incidents that he had apparently decided not to include in the final version. We didn't know where to insert them. So we did our best, realizing that the additions broke the flow of the rest of his narrative.

I can imagine something similar happening with the Gospel of John. The old man couldn't live much longer. His community wanted him to write down his stories of Jesus. So he did. But as he wrote, he got carried away with his theme of the conflict between Jesus and those he called "the Jews," even though everyone in the story was, in fact, a Jew – including Jesus.

Finally, he finished. But when the community read the manuscript, they cried out, "But you left out the story about…!"

So either old John wrote out a few of the extra favorite stories. Or else some of the people added the stories themselves, recalling the words they had heard from their mentor so many times. However it happened, they had some additional stories to insert into the manuscript.

And this is probably one of those insertions. It's here because it captures something of the personality of Jesus that Christians of that era wanted to ensure they remembered.

It's also the only reference in any of the gospels to Jesus writing anything. The story doesn't say what he wrote. Possibly, he simply doodled in the sand to stall for time.

But his reply was inspired. He turned the challenge around. Instead of pointing fingers outwards, toward the woman – and where, by the way, was the man with whom she was caught committing adultery? – Jesus forces the accusers to look inward, into their own actions and motivations.

And they faded away.

The Jewish law that prescribed stoning as a punishment for adultery also specified how the stoning should happen. Judgment required two witnesses. After the guilty person was tossed off a cliff, the two witnesses who laid the charge had the responsibility of crashing the first rocks down on the broken body below.

When those witnesses slipped away, there was no longer a case against the woman.

Whether it's a later insertion or not, the story belongs – because it dramatizes what Jesus has been doing with us ever since. Just when we think we have all the answers, he forces us to look inside ourselves, at our own actions and motivations.

Ponderings

- As you read this story, do you tend to take the side of the men, or the woman?
- Do you look for extenuating circumstances, when someone breaks a clearly defined law?
- Is justice always fair?

Prayer

I wish I could always have the compassion to care for the poor, the voiceless, the downtrodden. But I confess that there are times when I side with the existing power structures.

John 8:12–59
Not in lectionary
(8:31–36 ELC: Reformation Sunday, ABC)

If you leave out the story of Jesus and the woman caught in adultery (verses 1–11), John's recounting of Jesus' ongoing argument with the Pharisees continues as if it had never been interrupted. That is one reason why some literary critics treat the digression as a later insertion into John's narrative.

At the beginning of this series of verses, Jesus makes another of his "I am…" assertions: "I am the light of the world." It must have struck a raw nerve. The prophet Isaiah had described the nation of Israel as "a light to the world" (Isaiah 42:6 and 49:6). To his hearers, Jesus must have sounded as if he were usurping *their* role, *their* birthright. The more perceptive might have heard him reprising the Esau and Jacob conflicts from their own history, but switching roles, treating *them* as Esau, the one willing to squander his birthright, and taking the role of Jacob for himself.

No wonder, as the dialogue unfolds, they get huffy and remind him that they too are "descendants of Abraham" (verses 33 and 39).

They have some cause to feel huffy. Verse 31 tells us these are the Jews who believed in Jesus. But Jesus treats them roughly, almost harshly. From a relatively innocuous opening – "You will know the truth, and the truth will set you free," a statement that probably ought to be the slogan of the mainline churches in the same way that John 3:16 has become the slogan of the evangelical churches – Jesus ends up calling them the sons of the devil (verse 44)!

For me, the crux of this dialogue comes in verse 43: "Why do you not understand what I say?" I sense a frustration in his voice, almost a desperation. I've felt this myself when I have tried to say something as clearly as I can, and yet some people *still* miss the point – or worse, take my meaning as the opposite of what I had intended. So Jesus gets somewhat testy.

If that doesn't sound like the gentle-Jesus-sweet-and-mild you learned about years ago, remember that Jesus was human as well as divine, one of us as well as one with God. He got depressed. He got angry. All three of the other gospels describe him snapping at Peter, calling him "Satan," when Peter also failed to understand (Mark 8:33 and parallels).

Ponderings
- How do you react to the idea of Jesus getting angry, frustrated, or depressed? Can you accept a grumpy Jesus?
- How are you most likely to react when people misunderstand you?
- Have you ever deliberately tried to pick holes in someone else's assertions?

Prayer
I don't have to agree with everything that others say. But before I can know whether I agree or not, I have to hear them fully. Keep me from closing my mind to their words.

John 9:1–41
All: Lent 4, A

The parallels with healing stories in the synoptic gospels are obvious. But this one goes into more detail.

It's worth reading John's stories out loud. Because John, more than any other gospel writer, casts his characters as individuals. They are as real as the actors in any play – and like a play, reading the parts dramatically enhances our awareness of what's going on.

In this story, hear the disciples, baiting Jesus with theological riddles to get him to talk.

Hear neighbors, whispering to themselves behind their palms, trying to figure out if someone has pulled a fast one on them, and substituted a man who can see for the man who was blind from birth.

Hear the Pharisees conferring in confusion, testing the reality of their own eyes against the religious dogma that they dared not question (just as some today who will believe their own experience only if they can validate it through some biblical text).

See the man's parents, terrified of getting caught up in something they don't know about, wringing their hands, protesting their innocence. "Go talk to him yourself," they say.

Listen to the formerly blind man, resolutely sticking to his facts. "I don't know how he did it," he says. "All I know is, I was blind, and now I can see." Hear his frustration when his inquisitors pester him: "I told you once already! If you didn't believe me then, why would you believe me now?" Until finally, hounded into a corner, he's forced into an unwilling conclusion: "If this man were not from God, he could do nothing!"

And he was driven out. Not just from the Pharisees' court, but from the village. From the entire social order. He could see; he didn't have to be a beggar anymore; he could now earn a living. But exclusion dashed that hope.

And see Jesus, saddened that things had turned out wrong, seeking the man out.

The climax of this story, like any punch line, comes right at the end. "Are you trying to tell us that *we're* the blind ones?" some of the Pharisees demand.

"Memorizing the right answers," Jesus says, in effect, "is useless if you never ask questions."

Ponderings
- Have your good intentions ever turned out badly? Can you figure out what happened?
- Is it remotely possible that Jesus felt he had made a mistake?
- Are there people who take everything the wrong way? Are they "blind"?

Prayer
When I'm tempted to leap to conclusions, let me keep an open mind – especially when keeping an open mind might challenge some of my preconceptions.

John 10:1-10
All: Easter 4, A

This is another of Jesus' famous "I AM..." assertions. Here, he says not once but twice: "I am the gate."

This particular saying is less popular among mainline churches than his other "I am" sayings, because it seems – like Luke's "narrow gate" (Luke 13:24) – so exclusive. Jesus calls anyone who marches to a different drummer "a thief and a bandit" (verses 1 and 8). Combined with John 14:6 – "No one comes to the Father except by me" – it casts doubt on the current enthusiasm for interfaith dialogue and tolerance.

I wonder about the context in which Jesus made these statements. I'd like to think that Jesus intended them – like Paul's injunctions against women speaking in church (1 Corinthians 14:35) – as a response to immediate concerns, not as a general principle. (In fact, Paul simply repeated to the Corinthians the customary rules applied in synagogues.)

If it is true that God "makes [the] sun rise on the evil and on the good, and sends rain on the righteous and on the unrighteous" (Matthew 5:45), such a God will not deny the possibility of salvation to those who have never had the opportunity to know about and to follow Jesus as "the way, the truth, and the life." In his letter to the Romans, Paul has to go through intellectual gymnastics to prove that Jesus' own ancestor, Abraham, was not a discard onto the spiritual garbage heap. But if Abraham could be saved by faith, although it was not faith in Jesus Christ, should other devout seekers of God – whatever their faith tradition – be cut off by the narrow gate? Is God a racist? Is it only Abraham's bloodline that makes the difference?

As I read it, Jesus' primary purpose in this statement seems to be to warn against false prophets. "The people trust *me*" – we can almost hear his emphasis, contrasting himself to the false prophets – "because they *know* me." When his hearers don't get the message, he states his claim more emphatically.

It's a theme that John first introduced in chapter 5. "Don't trust your texts, or your traditions," Jesus says, in effect. "Trust *me!*" As Rabbi Jacob Neussner noted, this is the sticking point for devout

Jews. They might accept, even welcome, Jesus' teachings – many of which cut to the heart of their own ancient wisdom. But having learned to put their faith in God as revealed in the Torah (the first five books of what we patronizingly call the "Old Testament"), a faith that had kept their culture alive through 15 centuries of turmoil, they could not easily give up that faith and put it in a person instead.

Verse 10 contrasts Jesus' way with the way of the thief. This is much less exclusive than his image of the gate. The comparison implies that everyone is eligible for salvation if they devote their lives to making sure that others "may have life, and have it abundantly," and if they live according to Jesus' "way" of vulnerability, humility, and constant awareness of the presence of God.

Ponderings
- Do you deliberately choose your friends? Or do your friendships just happen?
- Have you ever rejected someone's friendship because that person didn't measure up to your standards?
- In what ways does your congregation create a "narrow gate" that excludes some individuals or groups of people?

Prayer
I love my friends, God. But help me remember that when I hug them, I turn my back to those outside the circle. Help me – help us – draw a wider circle.

John 10:11-18
All: Easter 4, B

Jesus gets more shocking. He takes the historic Hebrew metaphor for God, the metaphor of "the good shepherd," and applies it to himself. Not just once, which might be accidental, but twice he says, "I am the good shepherd."

It goes along with the other "I am..." claims found only in John's gospel, all of which attribute to Jesus qualities that were formerly reserved for God alone.

In this case, "shepherd" was one of the three most familiar divine metaphors: shepherd, king, warrior. David, of course, combined all three – one reason why he became the ideal for the Hebrew people. His son Solomon was, in worldly terms, a wealthier and more powerful king, but was neither shepherd nor warrior. Psalm 23 presents the shepherd image most powerfully. But there are numerous other parallels in the psalms and prophets.

Did Jesus really claim divine status? I don't know. Some modern scholars do not consider any of these sayings authentic. Authentic or not, I think they reflect the tradition of the storyteller. And a storyteller Jesus certainly was.

Storytellers depend on literary allusions. In our time, they may refer to gingerbread houses and wicked stepmothers, to fingers stuck in dikes and ninth-inning home runs. If I refer to Goldilocks or Cinderella, or, for that matter, to Mickey Mouse or the Roadrunner, most of my readers immediately catch the connection. They recognize the point I'm trying to make.

In Jesus' time and place, the primary literature was what we call the Old Testament. When he referred to vineyards and fig trees, seasons and shepherds, he counted on some of his hearers recognizing the allusions. They could put two and two together.

John's gospel includes seven sayings of Jesus that specifically use the words "I AM..." – although there are other instances that could be included, such as Jesus' reference to himself as the "living water" in John 4. These are the most commonly accepted seven:

John 6:35 and 51
I am the bread of life

John 8:12 and 9:5
I am the light of the world

John 10:7 and 9
I am the gate

John 10:11 and 14
I am the good shepherd

John 11:25
I am the resurrection and the life

John 14:6
I am the way, the truth, and the life

John 15:1 and 5
I am the true vine

So this is not just about how a dedicated shepherd will act. Nor is it simply a forecast of his forthcoming self-sacrifice. It's a piece of a puzzle that the writer of John's gospel puts together to build an unchallengeable case for the early church's first creed: "Jesus is Lord."

In the final verses of this passage, John introduces a theme that will figure more prominently in later chapters – the idea that Jesus "lays down his life" by his own choice. He is neither a victim of circumstances beyond his control, nor a robot sent by God to obey predetermined commands. Whether Jesus really knew what would happen or not, the theology of the early church is clear – Jesus acted voluntarily.

Ponderings

- Jesus made seven "I AM..." claims. What kind of picture do these pieces of a puzzle put together?
- Was Jesus boasting?
- How would you define yourself, if you started "I am..."?

Prayer

Jesus, trying to follow you is sometimes like chasing shadows on a wall. I wish I could see you more clearly.

John 10:22–30
All: Easter 4, C

According to the synoptic gospels, the adult Jesus made only one trip to Jerusalem, shortly before his crucifixion. That was at Passover time, in the spring. But in this reading, John clearly puts Jesus in Jerusalem during winter, attending the Festival of Lights that we call Hanukkah. Perhaps that's why he chose this occasion to call himself "the light of the world."

His critics challenged him to declare himself publicly, like a politician announcing he will accept a nomination. Jesus chose, instead, to teach a lesson about belief.

Psychology had not yet invented the term "self-justifying premise." It means that what we expect, we will see. But Jesus clearly understood the principle. "It wouldn't matter what I tell you," he chided his critics. "You wouldn't believe it anyway."

Then he repeated his allusion to himself as a shepherd with sheep. And he rubbed salt into the purists' wounds. He made the ultimate assertion: "The Father and I are one." Little wonder they picked up rocks to stone him (verses 31–33).

Reading through the four gospels, you can trace the early church's growing understanding of Jesus. In Mark, the earliest gospel, Jesus makes no extraordinary claims for himself. He calls himself the Son of Man, a euphemism translated elsewhere (in Ezekiel, for example) as "mortal." When people want to know if he is the Messiah; he refuses to acknowledge that title. He tells the demons and those he healed not to talk about him. He seems to prefer anonymity.

Later stories start to assert his divinity. By the time of Matthew and Luke, Jesus is more often described as the Son of God. Here in John, his own words seem to make him indistinguishable from God.

Or do they? The rest of the passage clearly distinguishes between Jesus and God; they are separate entities. He acts "in his Father's name." His sheep are God's gift, a gift that "no one can snatch out of the Father's hand." Some versions translate verse 39 as "My Father who has given them to me is greater than all."

If his "shepherd" identity is metaphoric, perhaps the "unity" in the same passage is also a figure of speech. Literary critic Northrop Frye called it "metonymy" – the identification of the whole with a part. The nation identified itself with its king (especially David) without thinking every citizen was entitled to live in a palace. All Hebrews identified themselves with Abraham, the patriarch who was long dead. It was a common idiom of the time.

It's possible that Jesus was simply saying, "I belong to God."

Not that his critics would hear it that way. They were looking for fuel, not for a fire extinguisher.

But we, who claim to be believers, should not necessarily read as literal fact words that may originally have been figurative.

Ponderings

- What kinds of groups (social, sports, business, ethnic, etc.) do you identify yourself with? What kind of words do you use to express that identification?
- Do you understand yourself better now than you did, say, 20 years ago? Will you allow the early church the same growth in understanding?
- Which matters more to you, at your present state of faith – Jesus' divinity, or his humanity?

Prayer

Jesus, all these arguments confuse me. Does it matter whether you are divine or human? Isn't it enough that you are simply you?

John 10:31–42
Not in lectionary

Jesus must have had more lives than a cat. Once again, his opponents turn into a lynch mob. They don't just *want* to stone him – they actually pick up the rocks to do it.

And Jesus traps them into a scriptural argument. They accuse him of blasphemy, of calling himself God. He quotes their own scripture back at them. Presumably, they're left in enough confusion, searching their own sacred texts to see if he was right, that Jesus was able to escape their clutches.

I confess to using this tactic myself, on occasion, when Jehovah's Witnesses have come ringing my doorbell. I forget the origins of the discussion, but one of the pair said something about God acting only through God's chosen people, the Jews.

"What about Cyrus the Persian?" I asked. "Didn't God also use him?"

Half an hour later, as they drove away, they were still chasing references to Cyrus in Chronicles, Ezra, Isaiah, and Daniel.

John doesn't tell us what happened to the would-be executioners. He simply says that Jesus left Jerusalem, and went down to the Jordan – a winter refuge for those who could afford a second home in the tropical valley. In that more relaxed setting, "many believed in him."

Ponderings
- What's the most difficult situation you've ever found yourself in?
- Do you know your Bible well enough to recognize some of its inconsistencies?
- When you're in a different setting, do you behave differently?

Prayer
I'm not like them, am I - nitpicking on details, finding excuses not to believe, being holier-than-thou in church settings?

John 11:1-45
All: Lent 5, A

The drama now starts to build towards its climax. John's narrative becomes more intense, more compelling - and, typically, more human.

The first part of this long reading (verses 1-31) sets up the second part (verses 32-45).

John is more than a collector of stories, like the writers of the other three gospels. Rather, John uses all the techniques of modern writers - dialogue, dramatization, foreshadowing - to make the ultimate conflict between Jesus and the authorities totally believable. John doesn't leave loose ends in his plot.

The crunch comes at verse 53: "From that day on they planned to put him to death." The rest of this chapter sets up this inevitable conclusion.

Notice the steps John takes. First, he introduces Lazarus' illness. He reminds his readers, through the disciples' reaction, that Jesus' life has already been threatened. So Jesus holds back. But after two days, he can no longer protect his own skin; he *has* to go to Jerusalem. Martha meets him - setting up a key discussion. Jesus gives another of his I AM sayings: "I am the resurrection and the life..." And Martha makes her great affirmation: "You are the Messiah, the Son of God, the one coming into the world."

Eventually, in response to the sisters' faith in him, Jesus raises Lazarus from the dead. And a lot of other people start to believe too.

That was the last straw. Raising people from the dead was affront enough, but the authorities said (verse 48), "If we let him go on like this, everyone will believe in him."

John sets up his story so that we can see the consequences coming. Once events have been set in motion, the countdown to the final curtain starts.

Ponderings
- Would you risk your life to help a friend?
- Does it take someone's illness or death to gather your family and friends together?
- Have you ever been backed into a corner, where you felt you had no alternatives open to you?

Prayer
Sometimes the things I do often have unexpected consequences. I can't help that. But I hope that those consequences never result from an action that I later regret.

John 11:32-44
RCL: All Saints, B

Mary must have had a better press agent than Martha. Mary gets praised for sitting at Jesus' feet doing nothing; Martha gets censured for providing hospitality (Luke 10:38-42). Martha has the dominant role in this story – actually a group of stories – but Mary gets the credit for bringing many Jews with her, who saw and believed.

Martha, in fact, plays the role that Peter often takes in the other gospels. All three of the other gospels tell of Peter's great confession. Jesus asks, "Who do you say that I am?" And Peter blurts out, "You are the Christ, the son of the living God" (Matthew 16:16 and parallels).

Here, that confession comes from Martha: "I believe that you are the Messiah, the Son of God" (verse 27).

Martha came out to meet Jesus; Mary stayed home.

Although Martha is the central character in this story, Lazarus grabs the headlines. Can't you imagine how the *National Enquirer* would relish it? "Man returns from dead! Flesh already rotting!" We flock to this story the morbid way some people are attracted to, say, pornography or violence, in videos or on the Internet. But it wasn't a unique story. If the Bible can be trusted – and if it can't, none of these stories are worth discussing – Jesus raised at least two others from death (Luke 7:11, Mark 5:35).

Lazarus's story differs mainly in Martha's protest: "He's been four days in there. Already, there's a stench!" Even if Lazarus wasn't fully dead when interred, four days without food or water would have finished him off.

That's what makes this the final, climactic event, as John develops the events foreshadowing Christ's trial, crucifixion, and resurrection. At the time, Jewish belief held that God separated body and soul after three days. Jesus demonstrated his divinity by having the power to re-unite what God had torn asunder.

But set aside the Twilight Zone, and is Lazarus in any way changed? Has he learned anything from his experience? If he does, the Bible makes no reference to it. The scriptural focus is on Martha and Mary. And clearly, Martha is the most affected by Jesus' visit.

So how come she gets the bad press?

Ponderings
- Imagine that a friend or family member came back from the dead. Would you rejoice? Or be terrified?
- How would your relationship with that person change? How would you treat that person differently?
- Are you jealous when someone else gets the credit for your efforts?

Prayer
I want to believe. I really do. I don't know what keeps holding me back. Lord, help my unbelief.

John 11:46–57
Not in lectionary

Here is the conclusion of the story, the fateful decision by the temple authorities.

The first reaction of any organization, when threatened, is to defend itself. In this sense, organizations act like any other organism – whatever their high ideals or lofty aims, their first priority is their own survival.

John may have had inside information about the priests' deliberations. Chapter 18:16 says that "the other disciple" – perhaps not the gospel writer himself, but certainly his source – "was known to the high priest" and was allowed into the courtyard, although Peter was kept outside.

Whether or not the words of Caiaphas are factually correct, they rationalize perfectly the attitude of any threatened organization: "It is better to have one man die for the people than to have the whole nation destroyed."

To this day, organizations sacrifice individual bodies to save the corporate body.

Ponderings
- Do you know anyone who was sacrificed by a business, corporation, or agency? Does the victim feel any better, knowing the sacrifice was for a worthy cause?
- When should privileged information be made public?
- Do you have responsibilities for looking after others? What would happen to them if you sacrificed yourself?

Prayer
Jesus, you sacrificed yourself. I know that I should be willing to sacrifice myself too. But it's hard to follow your example.

John 12:1-11
RCL & ELC: Lent 5, C (John 12:1-8)
RCL & ELC: Monday of Holy Week, ABC

A woman bursts into a gathering of men. That's shocking enough. Then she anoints Jesus with perfume worth a year's wages.

All four gospels tell this story in various ways. They don't agree on location: John calls it the house of Lazarus. Matthew and Mark call it the house of Simon the leper. Luke calls Simon a Pharisee and puts the incident earlier in Jesus' ministry. Matthew and Mark have the ointment going onto Jesus' head; Luke and John onto his feet. Luke starts with tears, the other three with ointment. John names the woman; the others don't.

But the essence of the story is the same. As Jesus says, in the *Good News* translation, "She has done a fine and beautiful thing for me" (Mark 14:6).

His disciples probably expected him to praise them, when they protested that the woman would have done more to further Jesus' mission if she had sold the ointment and given the money to them to distribute to the poor. (They sound a lot like a church mission or outreach committee.)

He didn't. As I wrote in *Last Chance* (Wood Lake, 1989, p. 62), "Many people give generously to support clothing stores and soup kitchens. But they wouldn't dream of getting to know a transient personally... They make compassion a *principle*; Jesus always made it a *person*."

The point, in the fewest possible words, is that someone cared about Jesus; and he was touched by it.

Whether Judas was a thief, or merely a bean-counter, is irrelevant. So is the argument, almost certainly added with the wisdom of hindsight, about Mary somehow anticipating the need to anoint Jesus' body. That interpretation, as *The Five Gospels* (Polebridge, 1993, p. 116) notes, "is possible only for those who already know the outcome of the gospel: Jesus dies, but he is raised before his body can be anointed..." following the delay required by the Sabbath.

In my Bible, chapter 12 with this story, and the story of Jesus washing the disciples' feet in chapter 13, are on facing pages. They would not have been in John's original manuscript. Nevertheless,

John is a skilled storyteller. I cannot imagine that John would not recognize the juxtaposition of the two stories.

Why would he choose to put these two stories so close together? Perhaps to remind readers that Jesus took for himself a task that his own disciples had scorned, not long before.

Ponderings
- What "fine and beautiful thing" has someone done for you? How, and why, did it move you?
- Did anyone misinterpret this gesture? Did their reaction cheapen it?
- If it's the little things in life that make a difference, why do you pay more attention to the grand (and expensive) gestures?

Prayer
Please, God, keep me sensitive to opportunities where I can do "a fine and beautiful thing" for someone else.

John 12:12–16
RCL & RC: Palm Sunday, B

As usual, the details vary, but all four gospels agree that Jesus rode a donkey into Jerusalem. John does not make it as deliberate a choice as the other gospels do. Here, it could occur almost by chance – Jesus happened upon a donkey on his way, and took it to ride on.

Typically, John shuffles the chronology. According to the other gospels, Jesus' choice of the colt comes first. *Then* he rode into Jerusalem. The sequence implies that his choice of a mount gave the crowds the clue that he was fulfilling Zechariah's prophecy (Zechariah 9:9), which, in turn, precipitated the mob scene that worried the Roman rulers.

John is, however, consistent with his own narrative. After the raising of Lazarus, John told us, many people believed in Jesus. These folks had already gone out to celebrate his arrival, noisily, *before* Jesus climbed onto the donkey.

I remember the first time I saw the world-famous Passion Play in Oberammergau, in the Bavarian Alps. In the opening scenes, hundreds of performers – even the children from the local schools –

spilled across the huge open air stage.

I had expected, somehow, that Jesus would stand out from the crowd. I didn't know how, but somehow I thought he might tower head-and-shoulders over the ordinary people, or glow, or have some distinguishing clothing like Superman. But he didn't. In that bedlam of people, there was only one way to pick out Jesus. He was the one on the donkey.

Ponderings
- Do you expect famous people to be larger than life?
- How would you recognize Jesus in a crowd?
- Can you think of any other reasons – other than a deliberate fulfilling of prophecy – why Jesus might have decided to ride on a donkey?

Prayer
Whenever I start feeling that I deserve a parade in my honor, remind me of what happened to Jesus in the days following Palm Sunday.

John 12:20-36
All: Lent 5, B (John 12:20-33)
RCL & ELC: Tuesday in Holy Week, ABC
(12:23-26 RC: All Souls, A)

John confirms my suspicions – people in biblical times didn't understand God's messages any better than we do. The Bible tends to make the word from heaven so explicit that we, in turn, tend to expect to receive instructions printed and proofread for errors or omissions.

In this passage, John even has Jesus carrying on a dialogue with the voice from heaven. But the crowd standing by thought they heard thunder. Or possibly an angel. The message was about as unintelligible to them as announcements over the public address system in most airports.

And Jesus himself doesn't seem to have much interest in clarifying things. A group of Greeks wanted to meet Jesus. They asked Philip to introduce them to Jesus. Philip would be a nominee for "best supporting actor" – he never gets a starring role, but he brings Nathanael to Jesus and evangelizes the Ethiopian diplomat.

Jesus was probably both thrilled and fearful – thrilled to receive recognition, fearful that this recognition would hasten the inevitable confrontation between his way and the way of the local authorities.

But when the crowd questions him, his responses seem almost obtuse. Even irrelevant. They ask who he is; he talks about light and darkness, about seeds falling into ground, about losing one's life to gain it.

With the benefit of hindsight, we can find meaning in his metaphors. But his hearers must have gone away shaking their heads.

Ponderings
- Have you ever had conversations that left you bewildered, feeling that you had missed the point somehow?
- Do you replay conversations in your mind, trying to make sense of them?
- In your experience, have good news and bad news often gone together?

Prayer
Sometimes, when I don't grasp the message immediately, I blame the other person for failing to communicate. Maybe it's also my own inability to listen.

John 12:37–50
Not in lectionary

Here is almost a cry of despair. Jesus flees from the dangers of Jerusalem. He retreats to safety. Because "they did not believe in him."

During the years after Jesus' death and resurrection, the church had plenty of time to pore over the only scriptures they had, looking for proof-texts to support their conviction that Jesus was indeed the long-promised Messiah. Of course, they found them – often in Isaiah.

Personally, I doubt that Isaiah intended these – or any other of his inspired figures of speech – to refer to Jesus. Isaiah was not a fortuneteller, forecasting the future from either chicken entrails or visions. Like the other prophets, he spoke about his own times. He slashed through the pretense and hypocrisy he saw around him; he recognized the inevitability of what would happen if people didn't change.

But there is little doubt in my mind that Isaiah influenced Jesus' own understanding of what it meant to be a Messiah. Sometimes I suspect that the child Jesus was brought up on Isaiah the way our children were brought up on *Sesame Street* or *The Flintstones*. Isaiah's powerful images of the nation of Israel as a suffering servant (Isaiah chapters 49-53) seem especially to have imprinted themselves in Jesus' self-consciousness.

The summary of Jesus' teaching (verses 44-50) contains a recurring theme of judgment. This is not a popular theme in our time. We prefer to focus on love and forgiveness. But obviously, it mattered to John.

Ponderings
- Do you expect to be judged for what you have and haven't done? When?
- Would it bother you to share "heaven" with a serial killer/rapist who only repented at the last moment?
- Have you forgiven your children (or your parents) for any suffering they caused you?

Prayer
Forgive me, God, for thinking that I can earn my way into eternal life.

John 13:1-17, 31b-35
All: Thursday in Holy Week, ABC
(For verses 31-35, see below.)

One of the great puzzles of the Bible – and one of the reasons why many biblical scholars treated John's gospel as less authentic than the first three – is why John failed to tell the full story of the Last Supper. For Matthew, Mark, and Luke, it was the culminating symbol of Jesus' ministry. Paul, writing his letters before any of the gospels, cites it as Jesus' most memorable act. Indeed, it is the *only* act performed by Jesus during his life that Paul mentions (1 Corinthians 11:23-26). Luke makes it the sign by which the disciples recognize their risen Lord (Luke 24:30-31).

But John ignores this story entirely. It's as unlikely as the Rolling Stones failing to perform their hits at a concert.

As a storyteller myself, I can imagine only two reasons for John to leave out the Last Supper.

First, it was already so well known that he didn't feel any need to tell it again. If communion had already become the central ritual of the early church, then the story would be told every time Christians gathered together. So John may have felt, "Why bother?"

Second, he may have wanted to change the emphasis of the church's practice. By the time John's gospel was written, the church had already created a fledgling pecking order of bishops, priests, deacons, and laity. Possibly the ordained leaders were already treating communion as their private preserve, a ritual over which they alone might preside. If so, John may have deliberately introduced this story to drive home, inescapably, the message that no one in Jesus' community enjoyed a privileged position.

If Jesus himself models the behavior he expects of his followers, it becomes harder for local leaders to slip into lordly postures.

Verse 13 sets up the theme of Jesus' final message to his disciples in chapters 14 through 19 – chapters which form his valedictory address. As a storyteller, here, John uses the technique of "foreshadowing." That is, he introduces a new idea, but without dwelling on it, so that his readers will be prepared when it comes back more forcefully.

So far, John's gospel has mainly stressed the unity of Jesus and God. Now, John begins to shift the emphasis to a larger unity. As Jesus, in his life, reveals God to his disciples, so they, in their lives, must reveal him to the rest of the world.

Ponderings

- Do you expect to get credit – or at least gratitude – when you do something for someone else?

- Do you resent being taken for granted – for example, when picking up after your family, cooking meals, maintaining appliances, handling routine tasks at work or at church?
- Does being a good example for others stimulate you? Or frighten you?

Prayer
Every minute of every day, I set an example for someone, somewhere. May it always be a good example.

John 13:21–32
RCL & ELC: Wednesday of Holy Week, ABC

All of the gospels agree that Judas betrayed Jesus. They don't agree, however, on how Judas came to his decision, nor on what happened to him afterward. But that probably doesn't matter, any more than it is necessary for all the witnesses to a car accident to agree on every detail of their testimony.

This is John's version of the betrayal. It assumes that one of the disciples – unnamed, but presumed to be young John – had inside information about Judas's intentions. But obviously, that knowledge was not communicated to the other disciples at the time. They still assumed that Judas had a position of responsibility among them as their treasurer.

In giving the piece of bread to Judas, Jesus re-enacted the ancient ritual of hospitality. Having broken bread together, host and guest were bound together. In Genesis, for example, Lot was obligated to protect the stranger in his home from a gang of local citizens (19:1–11). Judges 19 tells a similar story.

The symbolic gesture must have come like a slap in the face for Judas. I can see him recoiling from Jesus' offer, leaping back from the communal table, and rushing out into the night.

Ponderings
- If the favored disciple knew what was going to happen, and did nothing to prevent it, does that make him an accessory to the crime? Could the writer of John have offered this story as a kind of confession?

- Can you think of any acceptable excuses for Judas's actions?
- What rituals bind us together?

Prayer

I can do nothing of value by judging Judas. I can do something valuable only by ensuring that I do not follow his example, even unintentionally.

John 13:31–35
All: Easter 5, C

Once before, Jesus had summarized Jewish law into two commandments. Now, nearing the end of his earthly life, he gives his disciples a new commandment – to love one another the same way that he loved them.

A mere ten verses later, Jesus says, "I am the way... No one comes to the Father except through me" (John 14:6).

The expression is often interpreted exclusively to say that Jesus is the one and only door to salvation. Therefore, any other ways of believing or living must be eliminated and replaced with the Christian faith. The rationale has led us into cultural and social genocide against non-Christians. It launched the Crusades. It sent missionaries to impose a Western way of life and worship on "pagan" peoples. Here in North America, it uprooted aboriginal children and incarcerated them in residential schools. It encouraged settlers to wipe out native tribes.

But the commandment to love one another, which John clearly makes part of the same discourse, contradicts that exclusivity. How will people know these are his disciples? Not by a label on their T-shirts, nor by the creeds they affirm. Rather, the sign is that they love one another. That's what "my way" means. Jesus commends his own way of living and being to his disciples. Those who love each other, as he loved his friends, are his disciples – wherever they live, or whatever they call their God.

I'm a little surprised that the lectionary ignores verses 36–38. They're crucial to Peter's later denial of Jesus in the high priest's courtyard (John 18:15–27). William Barclay asks, "What was the difference between Peter and Judas?" Both failed him. Both regretted their betrayal or denial – according to Matthew 27:3–5, Judas felt so guilty he committed suicide. But Judas's name has become a curse, and Peter has turned into something like a lovable teddy bear.

Perhaps the difference is that Peter got a second chance to redeem himself; Judas didn't.

Ponderings

- Could devout followers of other faiths be Jesus' disciples, even if they have never heard of Jesus?
- Is Christianity worth believing, even if it is not the exclusive way to God?
- Is it possible to love someone else – to make allowances for their shortcomings, to sacrifice yourself for them – as much as you love yourself?

Prayer

I do try to love others. But my thoughts and wishes always return to myself. Teach me to be less self-centered.

John 14:1–14

All: Easter 5, A
(Also 14:1–17, ELC: St. Thomas, and
14:8–14 ELC: St. Philip and St. James)

There can be few more familiar passages in the gospels. It is read at most funerals – perhaps because verse 3 implies a purpose to death.

After my mother died, that thought comforted me. In our family, she tended to go first, to get the house or cottage ready for her family who would follow her. When she died before my father, it seemed natural to think of her going ahead, "to prepare a place…" In my grief, I was grasping at straws. But I thought of her doing like Jesus.

The late Henri Nouwen cited the rest of these verses as his spiritual manifesto when I interviewed him at his last residence, in the L'Arche home for severely handicapped persons north of

Toronto. Jesus expected his disciples to do everything that he had done (14:12) because they are one with him and with God (compare 17:21-23).

But for me, the cornerstone is verse 9: "Whoever has seen me has seen the Father." Too often, we start with some preconceptions about God, and then try to show how Jesus corresponds to them. Thus we insist that Jesus must have known exactly what was going to happen him – because God is omniscient. And that he could have rescued himself, but chose not to – because God is omnipotent.

My father, W.S. Taylor, suggested in a little book called *Seeing the Mystery* (which never received the attention I thought it deserved) that we may have come at God backwards. We have tried to define, *a priori*, the qualities that God must have: omnipotence, omniscience, love, judgment, authority... And then we have tried to show how Jesus demonstrated those "divine" qualities.

Sometimes, we bend the story to make it show what we think it ought to. So sermons portray Jesus' encounter with the Syro-Phoenician (or Canaanite) woman as a test of her faith rather than a story about Jesus' growing understanding of his ministry. Simple acts of kindness get turned into fulfillment of abstruse prophecy. And we never allow Jesus to have a bad day.

But maybe, my father suggested, we should look first at the qualities of Jesus, and apply them to God. That places no external expectations on Jesus – we see him solely as himself.

That might sound arrogant, except that he goes on: "And what I am, you will be." That's not arrogant. It's terrifying. And exciting. If we're willing to accept the challenge.

Perhaps we should start at the other end. "Whoever has seen me," Jesus says, "has seen the Father." What we know of Jesus tells us as much as humans are capable of knowing about what God is like.

Ponderings
- What qualities do you attribute to God? Would you be disappointed if Jesus did not always share those qualities?
- What adjectives would you use to describe Jesus? Do any of them contradict your ideas about God?

- Which of your qualities might reveal something about the nature of God?

Prayer

I make excuses for myself, God. I tell others, "I'm only human, after all." Don't let me underestimate myself.

John 14:8-17 (25-27)
All: Pentecost, C

This lectionary reading overlaps the Easter reading above, and therefore continues the same message. It states the doctrine of the Incarnation – the embodiment of God in a human – as forcefully as any of the birth narratives.

This time it's Philip, not good old doubting Thomas (John 20:24-29), who acts as foil. "Show us the Father," says Philip, "and we'll believe."

"God is like me," Jesus tells Philip. "Here I am. You know me. So you know what God is like."

The added verses (15-17 and the optional 25-27) introduce John's portrayal of God's holy spirit as "the Advocate." That's why this passage is read at Pentecost.

Verse 12 reiterates Jesus' promise that his disciples will emulate him: "The one who believes in me will also do the works that I do…" In the computer world, one program can "emulate" another program if it can do the same tasks and functions, even though the two programs may come from differing sources, and run under different operating codes. We don't have to be identical to Jesus to emulate him.

Ponderings
- Would you really want to be like Jesus?
- What kind of pain, or hurt, or loss, might that lead to? What kind of joys?
- Do you have to wear sandals to be like Jesus?

Prayer

Given a choice, I'd prefer comfort and luxury to suffering and heartbreak. But I know I must accept the worst, as well as the best, if I am truly to follow Jesus.

John 14:15-21
All: Easter 6, A

John's gospel devotes five chapters to Jesus' final message to his disciples. Whether Jesus actually said all these things, or whether his followers put them together later, convinced that he *must* have said them, is immaterial. We can take guesses – educated guesses from biblical scholars, gut hunches from the rest of us – but we can never know.

As one who has difficulty remembering a half-dozen items on a grocery list, I have trouble believing that any person without a tape recorder could accurately recall all 2766 words of Jesus' "valedictory address" for 70 years before writing them down. But that doesn't matter. Because this is what we have, and have had for 20 centuries, and it is foundational to Christian faith.

In this passage, Jesus promises something new and unprecedented to replace him when he has gone. The "Advocate" will help the disciples through difficult times, just as Jesus had. (Other translations of the Greek word *paraclete* come out as "helper" or "comforter.") John does not portray this "Advocate" as a separate entity. Verse 18 implies that it is Jesus himself, returning. So does the letter also attributed to John, 1 John 2:1.

John, and John alone of the gospel writers, uses the term "Advocate" – one who will plead a cause. But John didn't invent the idea. That understanding of the Spirit clearly influenced the early church. It threads through Paul's Epistles. Paul writes to the Romans (8:26) that "the Spirit *intercedes*…" And Peter's first letter visualizes baptism, the conferring of the Spirit, as "an *appeal* to God…" (1 Peter 3:21).

The Advocate takes our side. It must have been a comforting thought, especially when persecution of Christians grew more severe. As Paul said, "If God (Christ/the Spirit) is for us, who can be against us?" (Romans 8:31).

Ponderings
- How have you felt when someone you looked up to – a parent, teacher, elder, mentor – left you to undertake a difficult task on your own?
- Did you yearn to have that person take over, to rescue you?
- How do you know something is real if you can't recognize it with your physical senses?

Prayer
God, I'm grateful that you didn't leave us alone, that you shared your spirit with us. Help me recognize that spirit's presence in my daily life.

John 14:23-29
All: Easter 6, C
(14:21-27 ELC: St. Simon and St. Jude)

Jesus' discussion of the Advocate continues. Jesus describes the Holy Spirit in much the same terms that John the Baptist had used to describe Jesus. "The one who is coming after me," says the Baptist. "The one whom the Father will send," says Jesus. Both descriptions look ahead, to one who will complete what the other started.

Although the gospels are about Jesus, the New Testament as a whole is about the new church. The scriptures came out of the church, not the church out of the scriptures. Without the Holy Spirit, there would be no church. Little wonder the Holy Spirit becomes the culmination of all that went before.

Verse 31 introduces an interesting note. "Get up," Jesus says to the people at his farewell dinner. "Let's be on our way." But then he continues talking for three more chapters (15-17). So did he continue his discourse en route to Gethsemane (18:1)? Or is this a later addition, like the story of the woman caught in adultery? I'm inclined to think that John's original manuscript leaped from the end of chapter 14 to the beginning of chapter 18, and that the intervening three chapters resulted from John's community protesting that he had left out a lot that they had grown accustomed to discussing and studying.

Ponderings
- Have you experienced the presence of a spirit in your life?
- Are there bad spirits as well as good ones? How do you know the difference?
- What qualities would others identify in your spirit?

Prayer
At times I feel hopelessly inadequate. Let me always remember that I do not have to depend on my abilities alone.

John 15:1–8
All: Easter 5, B

The first of three chapters devoted entirely to Jesus' theological ruminations starts with another of his "I AM…" sayings. He compares his relationship to his disciples with the stem and branches of a vine.

Usually, we derive two points from this passage:
1. Pruning is good for the vine. A pruned vine produces more grapes than a wild one. Thus we justify both discipline and pain. It's for our own good, we profess – especially if we are imposing the discipline or inflicting the pain, however reluctantly.
2. Branches thrive only when connected to the main stem. The stem has lived longer than the branches. Thus we defend the church and its dogmas; we stifle doctrinal dissent as cutting oneself off from the main stem.

I've read this passage so often, I'm surprised I found anything new in it. But I did – the implication that a branch can choose whether or not it will be pruned.

But Jesus' words here – if we accept John's narrative at face value – are clearly not *about* the church, but *to* the church. Jesus speaks *to* the branches who will eventually become the church. And he urges them to "abide in him." To stay attached. Not to be the branches pruned off and cast into the fire.

How does a branch do that? Isn't the decision about pruning up to the pruner? In this case, to God?

Apparently not. Granted, it's possible to push any metaphor too far. But this one seems to have a clear implication here that the branches can influence their own fate. If they bear much fruit, they will not be burned.

The metaphor would resonate for Jesus' Jewish contemporaries. Isaiah, Jeremiah, Ezekiel, and Psalms all refer to Israel as a vine or a vineyard (Isaiah 5:1-7, Jeremiah 2:21, Ezekiel 19:10, Psalm 80:8). Jesus himself uses the image in his Parable of the Tenants in the Vineyard (Matthew 21:33-41, Mark 12:1-8, Luke 20:9-16). Curiously, all of these are negative references. They all imply that the vines, or the vine keepers, have failed to do their duty.

Against that background, Jesus' admonition conveys extra urgency. His followers dare not just to sit there like bumps on a pew. However they do it – by speeches, good works, or any of the other "fruits of the Spirit" – they are expected to produce. To live their faith, daily. That's the test of their attachment to the vine.

Ponderings
- What experiences of "pruning" have you had? What did you lose? What, if anything, did you gain?
- How did you feel towards the "pruner" – the person or situation that did the "pruning"?
- Do you wince in sympathy when you prune plants?

Prayer
In this individualistic culture, I'm constantly tempted to create my own private spirituality. I need to keep connected to the community of Jesus' followers.

John 15:9-17
All: Easter 6, B

Jesus gives his disciples a new commandment, based on love.

If you were to ask almost any contemporary Christian with some biblical literacy about Jesus' commandments, you'd probably get one of these answers, depending on the respondent's theological hue:
- To love God with all your heart and soul and mind and strength, and to love your neighbor as yourself (Matthew 22:37-39; Mark

12:29-31). (In Luke 10:25-28, the commandment comes from the lawyer, not from Jesus.)
- To do unto others as you would have them do unto you (Matthew 7:12; Luke 6:31).
- To make disciples of all nations (Matthew 28:19).

The third reads to me like an epilogue, a commissioning and benediction practiced by the early church and grafted onto the end of Matthew's gospel. The first two are probably authentic. But neither is original. The first is a summary of the Law of Moses, the traditional view of Judaism. The second was an adaptation of a saying also attributed to Rabbi Hillel, who lived shortly before Jesus. Hillel put the Golden Rule in the negative: "What you would not want others to do to you, do not do to them."

The commandment that John gives us, though, belongs uniquely to Jesus. It comes at the end of his ministry, when he has had time to reflect on his own message, like a last will and testament. It focuses on his own personal example – "that you love others as I have loved you" (verse 12).

I wonder why we do not give it precedence over the other commands.

Perhaps the problem starts in verse 9: "As the Father has loved me, so have I loved you." By implication, we have to love not just as Jesus loved, but as God loves.

Is this kind of love, perhaps, unthinkable, unimaginable? But if we don't try, isn't that a cop-out, a deliberate rejection of Jesus' final wishes for us?

Ponderings
- If Jesus is God, is it blasphemous even to think of being like him?
- From your reading of the Bible, what other commands or instructions from Jesus can you recall?
- Do you think Jesus liked everyone? Does God like everyone?

Prayer
Okay, I will try to love others. But I'm not sure that I can always like them.

John 15:18–26
Not in lectionary

I'm not surprised that the lectionaries chose to leave this passage out. It's a bleak passage, a passage about despair and hatred and suffering.

Perhaps it's appropriate that it follows the much more familiar – and more comfortable – metaphor of vines and pruning. Perhaps it suggests how that pruning may take place.

But there must have been some consolation to a church suffering persecution by Roman authorities to know that that they were not alone. "If the world hates you," John has Jesus saying, "be aware that it hated me too."

Ponderings
- Do you need to be liked and respected?
- How much of your integrity do you sacrifice to achieve that goal?
- How do you react when you experience hostility, when you feel you're being picked on?

Prayer
I don't want to be hated. And having your company, Jesus, doesn't make it any easier, because you're safely out of their reach, and I'm not.

John 15:26–27, 16:4b–15
All: Pentecost, B

John's gospel refers to the Holy Spirit, which Jesus promised would come to his disciples, as the "Advocate."

John's choice of title intrigues me. It cannot be an accident. By the time of John's gospel, Paul's letters had been in circulation for almost 50 years; the Acts account of Pentecost, for about 20 years. So John must have known the term "the Holy Spirit." Yet he claims Jesus used a different term – in Greek, *paraclete*, usually translated to mean counsel for the defense, advocate, or intercessor. Either he knew what Jesus actually said better than other writers, or he had some specific purpose in giving the Spirit another name.

I have a hunch that by the end of the 1st century, the doctrine of the Trinity may have begun to solidify. And John didn't particularly like it. Luke's version, in Acts, places a seven-week separation between Jesus' resurrection and the coming of the Holy Spirit. That separation almost inevitably led Christians to think of the Trinity as three distinct entities – God, Jesus, and the Holy Spirit.

So John deliberately chooses a different term. In John 14:16, Jesus had identified himself as an advocate with God for his followers. During his life, he counseled, guided, and interceded for his disciples. Perhaps John wants to indicate that the living Jesus, the risen Christ, and the Holy Spirit are one and the same.

Ponderings
- Do you normally pray to God, to Jesus, or to the Holy Spirit?
- How does Jesus function as an "advocate" in your life?
- Do you separate the various components of your life from each other? Which boxes do you keep your faith in?

Prayer
Whoever you are, God, don't let me ever start to think of you as something I can define and control.

John 16:12–15
All: Trinity, C

The verses chosen for this particular Sunday's lectionary reading don't interest me. They simply re-affirm what Jesus has already said about the Advocate.

I find the omitted and ignored verses 16–33 (not in the lectionary) much more interesting.

The prescribed reading cuts off immediately before a story about the disciples' confusion. None of the gospels – to their credit – minimize the disciples' inability to understand their leader. Over and over, the disciples miss the point.

Only John's gospel records this final fumble. With the 20/20 vision of hindsight, we understand that Jesus is foretelling his death, resurrection, and ascension. To his disciples, it sounds like verbal sleight of hand – "now you see me, now you don't." But they've been hurt by their failures too often already. They don't want to expose themselves once more as slow learners. So they talk to themselves, instead of to Jesus.

But he sees the signs. So he explains anyway.

Finally, in verse 25, he drops the metaphors. He puts his message in plain language.

And the disciples sigh with relief. So, I suspect, do most of us.

Ponderings

- Do you find yourself wishing, sometimes, that Jesus would quit beating about the bush and lay it on the line?
- Is the problem that his metaphors are not yours? Did you have any trouble understanding the metaphors in the previous question?
- How would you express Jesus' words, in this chapter, in plain language? Could you condense his message to 25 words or less?

Prayer

Sometimes I need to say things straight; sometimes I need to soften my words. The problem is to know when to do which.

John 17:1-11
All: Easter 7, A

Throughout the gospel, John has planted clues. "My time has not yet come," Jesus says, in various ways, over and over. But now we know the final act of the drama is near. "The hour has come," Jesus says.

In chapter 17, Jesus shifts gears. He confers his final blessing on his disciples. His story still has a climax to unfold. But this is his last chance to teach them.

His definition of eternal life (verse 3) makes no mention of life after death. Eternal life means to know God, and to know God's human revelation, Jesus himself. That's sufficient.

And his ultimate wish? The recurring theme of John's gospel – unity. "That they may be one, even as we are one." The unity of

Jesus with God; the unity of his disciples with himself. There's no room here for a compartmentalized life. Jesus pleads with God on his disciples' behalf, just as he has previously claimed the Advocate would.

These are almost certainly not Jesus' own words, if only because none of the disciples knew shorthand. If you really think that they could memorize this speech, and then regurgitate it word for word, some 50 years later, after just a single hearing, at a time when their minds were preoccupied with other things, then see how long, and how many repetitions, you would need to memorize it yourself. They were, in fact, in no condition to memorize anything. They were in shock. They had just learned – or it had finally dawned on them – that they were going to lose their friend, their leader.

When a doctor delivers a diagnosis of cancer, patients' minds shut down. They hear the words, the instructions, the reassurances. But all that registers is "cancer." The rest of the information needs to be written out, or remembered by another person, or transmitted in a second visit.

On the other hand, whether or not these are Jesus' exact words, I don't doubt at all that the early church believed that these words accurately reflected Jesus' intent.

Ponderings
- Does it bother you to have the church put words in Jesus' mouth?
- Have you ever understood someone's motivations too late, only after they've gone?
- Can individuals speak on behalf of a whole organization, or do they only speak for themselves?

Prayer
When I near the end of my life, I hope that my friends and family will want to hear the wisdom I have to offer them.

John 17:6-19
All: Easter 7, B

I met the late Henri Nouwen once, during a visit to Daybreak, the L'Arche home north of Toronto. He talked for over an hour, one to one, mostly about John 17. It was the centerpiece of his theology. The author of *The Wounded Healer* and about 20 others books summarized Jesus' theme in two short sentences: "What I have done, you will do. What I have been, you will be." The unity of Christ and his followers was more than symbolic – it was a handing on of the torch, a passing of the baton. They were to become him. They were to take his place.

This may be an unusual request, but it is a common desire on the part of survivors. Most people have, without realizing it, attempted to do this after the death of a loved one. My mother, for example, wrote regular letters to every relative. She kept track of everyone's birthday and anniversary. After she died, my father and I thought we could take her place. We kept records of birthdays and anniversaries. For several years, we dutifully sent cards. We wrote letters.

We didn't succeed, of course. We couldn't replace her. But in ways that we hadn't expected, we were changed by our efforts. We did not lose touch. We maintained contacts that formerly we had left to her.

Perhaps the effort is all that Jesus expects of us, too.

Ponderings
- Whose place have you attempted to take? When?
- Does the prospect of playing understudy to Jesus terrify you, or excite you?
- If you had a final prayer, what would you pray for?

Prayer
I know I can't take Jesus' place. But perhaps I can offer tiny glimpses of what he might be like.

John 17:20-26
All: Easter 7, C

Most of Jesus' prayers were short. Many are simply a sentence of blessing or a few words of entreaty. What we call "The Lord's Prayer" is a masterpiece of terseness, without a superfluous word – even if several of its elements come directly from a traditional Jewish evening prayer.

But this one – Jesus' great prayer for unity – takes an entire chapter. Every word is significant. Every sentence could be analyzed, and benefited from.

But for me, the key lines are in verses 21-22: "As you, Father, are in me and I in you, may they also be in us... that they may be one, as we are one."

Here, in modern idiom, the rubber meets the road. If we truly believe that Jesus and God are one, and indivisible, then – according to John – our own theology demands that we treat all other believers as one with us. But if we think of Jesus and God as two separate entities, then we will almost certainly transfer that conviction to our relationship with other persons.

And vice versa. If we make distinctions between ourselves and those of different origins, or status, or convictions, we probably also make a distinction between Jesus and God.

It's an equation that inextricably links God, Jesus, and all of us. John's wording seems designed to paint us into a corner.

I sense a fear in our churches of being like Jesus. Emulating Jesus might call us to be unpopular. It might involve risk. It might even involve getting crucified – though not necessarily on a cross. We try to avoid that possibility by treating Jesus as different from us. He was divine; we excuse ourselves by shrugging, "I'm only human."

But that's just as much a betrayal of Jesus' last wishes as Peter's denials by the bonfire.

Ponderings
- What would your last wish be?
- How would you summarize the message of your life?
- Are you more likely to notice your similarities to other people, or your differences?

Prayer

Sometimes I set my ideals too high, and then make excuses when I can't reach them. Instead of giving up on ideals, I need to set realistic goals for myself.

John 18:1 – 19:42
All: Good Friday, ABC

The lectionary occasionally sets very long passages. You may be tempted to skip this one, or to break it up into shorter units (as I have done in this book, in the pages that follow). Don't.

The first time I saw the Passion Play at Oberammergau, I knew the gospel stories thoroughly. But as the story unfolded, piece-by-piece, I found myself caught up in it. I had a sense of a juggernaut carrying an innocent victim along to an inexorable end. I wanted to leap up, to rush onto the stage, to shout, "Stop! Don't do it!"

No reading will have the same dramatic impact as a stage performance, of course. But reading the whole story has its own power.

Breaking the complete story of Jesus' arrest, trial, and crucifixion into smaller bits is like dissecting a butterfly. You may get more detailed knowledge about its component parts – but you'll never see it fly.

John 18:1–32
All: Part of Good Friday, ABC

We have several scenes in this single reading.

First, Jesus and the disciples go to a garden in the Kidron Valley. John does not call it Gethsemane; neither does Luke, though Matthew and Mark do. Nor does he tell the story of Jesus taking his three favorite disciples with him while he prayed: "Let this cup pass from me… Nevertheless, not my will but yours…" We might expect John to have eye-witness details that the other writers could not have known. But he doesn't mention it at all.

That leaves several possibilities. Perhaps, like the Last Supper, the story was already so well known that John saw no need to repeat it. Perhaps John really did sleep through the whole thing, and refused to pass along stories that he could not personally affirm. Or possibly the story was, like the stories of Jesus' birth, later creations of the church. Twenty centuries later, we cannot know.

Second, the high priests' hired guns arrest Jesus. If Judas had merely given the temple authorities information about Jesus, it might be possible to suggest that he was tricked, duped into revealing damaging facts. But by physically leading the mercenaries to Jesus, Judas removed any reasonable doubt about his intentions.

Third, Jesus refuses to save himself. He could have run away. He didn't. Not once, but twice, he says, "I am he. I am the one you want. Take me."

Fourth, Peter shows that he still hasn't got it. He still takes his wisdom from the ways of the world – precisely what Jesus criticized him for in Mark 8:33. He resorts to violence to solve problems. He uses his sword.

The story now quick-cuts, like a movie, between two settings. Inside, the priests grill Jesus. Outside, the hired help grill Peter. As usual, Peter comes off worst. Jesus retains his dignity even while being humiliated; Peter lies to protect his own skin. Not just once, but three times. Like Judas leading the temple cops to Jesus, the repetition eliminates any possibility that Peter might have been misquoted the first time.

Finally, Jesus is taken to Pilate, the only person who has authority to execute him. I've never seen an explanation of how the gospel writers knew what went on in Pilate's private chambers. One of the disciples apparently had access to the high priest's house (verse 15). But the Bible states clearly that not even the high priests went into Pilate's headquarters (verse 28).

Yet the give and take between Pilate and Jesus has the ring of reality. There's scorn in Pilate's voice, contempt for this pathetic nation he's stuck with governing. There's patient weariness in Jesus' voice as he attempts explanations that he knows Pilate cannot comprehend.

"What is truth?" Pilate shrugs, closing the conversation. I don't hear this as an openness, let alone a yearning, to hear the truth. It sounds more like jaded cynicism.

If this conversation is accurate, it could only have been passed on by Jesus himself. And only after his resurrection.

There was some urgency about getting Pilate to pass sentence. Assassination, murder, mugging – these were commonplace enough in those days. But they weren't enough. They could provoke a backlash. They might make the victim into a martyr. The temple authorities needed something more decisive, more final. They wanted to humiliate the man who had made them look foolish. He had to be remembered as nothing more than a common criminal.

Ponderings

- Has someone wronged you? How do you know it was intentional?
- When someone criticizes you, are you more likely to react like Peter or Jesus?
- Do you celebrate when someone who has harmed you is humiliated?

Prayer

When events conspire against me, when situations beyond my control overwhelm me, may I at least remain in control of myself.

John 18:33-37

All: Reign of Christ/Christ the King, B
RC: Sacred Heart, B

When Pilate asked Jesus, "Are you a king?" he couldn't understand Jesus' answer. Neither can we, because we constantly confuse the notion of "king" with territorial authority.

Canadians have a slight advantage here – at least they have a monarch to relate to, if distantly. Americans, on the other hand, founded their republic on a rejection of any monarchy – which makes their affirmation of Jesus' kingdom in worship at least a bit schizophrenic.

In the United States, this confusion shows up as an obsession with national security – no one's going to fool around on *our* turf. Canadians are more likely to identify themselves with the north's wide-open spaces, even though most of them live in a narrow strip along their southern border. Either way, a fixed focus on territory blinds us to other possibilities.

A kingdom is not measured with survey stakes. Nor is it marked by border patrols and customs offices. A kingdom depends on allegiance. You belong to whatever you commit your allegiance, your loyalty. So you are still married when you're not at home, a teacher when you're not in school, an American when you're in France or Malaysia. And when you meet a compatriot – overseas, or in another setting – you feel an instant bond.

British philosopher John Macmurray suggested, in a BBC radio talk, that the kingdom of God was like friendship. Jesus talked about things we know, he said. And among things we know, only friendship fits Jesus' description of something that is already among us, that we all long for, and that could happen anytime. And wouldn't that be a wonderful place, he asked, where everyone was a friend?

That's the kind of kingdom Jesus spoke of. He modeled it himself. His disciples followed his example, and patterned their behavior on his.

That's what Jesus meant when he said, "My kingdom is not like those of this world."

But Pilate, accustomed to thinking only of territorial authority enforced by the military might of the Roman Empire, couldn't understand. Nor, I fear, can we – until we set aside some preconceptions about kingship.

Ponderings

- To how many different levels of government ("rulers") do you pay taxes?
- To what causes or organizations do you give allegiance?
- Do you ever wish you could have just one clear authority in your life?

Prayer

It would be heavenly, if I could find common ground, let alone true friendship, with everyone I encounter.

John 19:1-42
The rest of Good Friday, ABC

This is the rest of the long passage prescribed for Good Friday. It is not often read in the lectionary. Yet the details – the crown of thorns, the purple robe, the screaming mob, the crosses, the inscription, the broken legs – are all too familiar.

John does no quick cuts between alternating scenes here. The sequence flows linearly. Jesus is bounced back and forth, before Pilate, before the mob, before Pilate, before his accusers... Eventually, the temple authorities out-maneuvered Pilate. "If you don't crucify him," they said, "we'll spread rumors about your own lack of loyalty to the Emperor."

Even a rumor would be the kiss of death for Pilate's chances of promotion. So he gave in. But first he stuck a sharp little knife into his antagonists. He forced fundamentalist Jews to perjure themselves, by pledging allegiance to an alien emperor.

And then he twisted the knife by putting up an inscription, "The King of the Jews." They could not miss the implication – a criminal king does not rule over honest folk, but over other crooks. No wonder they protested.

Of the four gospel writers, John takes the hardest stance against "the Jews." His bitterness reminds me of some divorced spouses I've met, who can find absolutely nothing good to say about their former partners.

In fact, that's not a bad analogy. Because Jesus didn't set out to create a new religion – he set out to revitalize an old one. Strange as it may seem, Jesus was never a Christian! He was a Jew, who lived and died among Jews, and it was among those Jews that he found the disciples who continued to proclaim his message. That's why Paul, in his travels around the eastern Mediterranean, first took his message to the Jewish synagogues.

By the time of this gospel, though, Christians were Jewish outcasts, as despised and rejected as the Samaritans. Trapped between the Roman rock and the Jewish hard place, John's persecuted Christian community lashed out at the folks who *ought* to have been their friends. Because they didn't expect anything better from the Romans, the Roman forces get off relatively lightly.

I have trouble with Jesus doing things "to fulfill prophecy" (verses 24 and 36-37). It makes him not much more than a jukebox playing pre-recorded tunes. More likely, a grieving community searched for solace in their historic scriptures, and found a few references that gave them, at least, some comfort. If this tragedy was pre-ordained, they could not have prevented it. Therefore they need not feel guilty.

Ponderings
- How do you put pressure onto people to get your way? How do you respond when people put pressure on you?
- Did you have any of those guilty "if only" feelings after the loss of someone you loved?
- God gave humans the gift of free will. Did God also give Jesus the right to make his own decisions?

Prayer
I know that dislike sometimes affects the way I think about some people. But I can at least try to be fair.

John 19:38-42
RCL: Saturday of Holy Week, ABC

This passage, like Holy Saturday itself, provides transition.

As a narrative, the gospel has to move us from Friday and the crucifixion, to Sunday and the resurrection. So Jesus has to be taken down from the cross, and put away where he can be kept on ice, so to speak, through the Jewish Sabbath.

All four gospels credit Joseph of Arimathea with providing a tomb for Jesus. Tombs were carved from solid rock, with just enough space for the family. Family had high value in Jewish society. For Joseph to put Jesus into that tomb meant depriving some member of his own family of a burial place – perhaps himself.

Only John's gospel includes Nicodemus in this transition story. This is Nicodemus' third appearance on stage. Though it's a bit part, he shows character development. The first time, Nicodemus doesn't want to be identified with Jesus, so they meet at night. The second time, Nicodemus speaks up for Jesus among his accusers – though not very forcefully. This time, he's out in the open. He helps to remove the body. He provides spices. He handles the body – which would have left him ritually unclean for his priestly duties – and helps to place it in a tomb.

Ponderings
- Do you expect Jesus to be successful every time?
- How have you included Jesus as a member of your family?
- How public are you about your faith in Jesus?

Prayer
I have Easter Saturdays in my life too – times when everything seems to be on hold. It helps to remember that they precede Resurrection Sundays.

John 20:1-18
All: Easter, ABC
RC: All Souls, C
ELC: St. Mary Magdalene, ABC

This is such a significant passage, it deserves several looks.

One approach
The writer of John makes events personal. In describing the Resurrection, Matthew cites fulfillment of prophecy, accompanied by lightning, thunder, and earthquakes, and supernatural voices. Mark and Luke give overviews. John tells the story from a human viewpoint.

In John's story, Mary came to the garden early in the morning. She couldn't wait to get there, so she started on her way even before dawn, during the darkness when grave robbers operated.

She found the tomb empty.

Appalled, terrified that grave robbers had done a final indignity to her beloved friend, she raced back down the hill to tell others.

She found Peter and the other disciple, generally assumed to be John himself. To their credit, they didn't scoff. They didn't, as in Luke's version of this story, consider her news to be "idle tales" (Luke 24:11). Instead, they ran to the tomb.

Running was undignified for Jewish males. The father of the prodigal son disgraced himself, in society's eyes, by running to meet his wayward child. But the two disciples ran. Through the streets, up the hill, to the tomb.

The other disciple was younger, and ran faster than Peter. But he lacked Peter's brash confidence. So he stopped at the entry to the tomb. Peter, typically, barged right in. And the other disciple followed.

The message may be literally factual, or it may be hindsight, a parable of the way people come to faith. Some come to it cautiously, some blunder into it.

A second approach

In John's version of the resurrection story, Mary Magdalene is the first to see the risen Christ.

Jesus' closest female relationship seems to have been with Mary. Three possibilities exist: that they were married, that they were lovers, that they were simply very close. Whichever one you prefer to believe, she has to be the woman who felt his loss most deeply.

Mary knew Jesus was dead. She had gone to anoint his decaying body with spices. And the body was gone. Her first reaction must have been livid anger. It wasn't enough that they had hung this man on a cross to die. It wasn't enough that he had to be laid in a borrowed tomb. Now grave robbers had stolen his body, before she could complete the last rites of love. Would these indignities never end?

Alone in the garden, she breaks down and cries her heart out. Through her tears, she sees someone. Maybe he knows where she can find the body, where she can hold it one last time. She appeals to this person, whoever he is. And through her tears she hears his voice say her name: "Mary!"

Ralph Milton, David Jones, and I all lost sons. They were all in their early 20s at the time. We would have given almost anything to hear that vanished voice say once more, "Dad!" Our hearts would have turned cartwheels within us.

Mary's did.

A third approach

I have never heard a sermon on the rolling away of the stone from the *inside*. Mary stands outside, weeping. John bends down and looks in. Peter actually goes in. But the perspective is still from the outside, looking in.

But what would one see from the inside, looking out? Was it pitch dark in there, the stygian lightlessness of the underworld? When the stone across the door began to move, did a slim crescent of light appear, like the first new moon in the sky?

What was it like for Jesus, to realize that his faith in a loving God had not been in vain after all? He had staked his life on that faith. In that terrible final cry, "My God, my God, why have you forsaken me?" (Mark 15:34) did the human in him wonder if he had been wrong?

And then, in the darkness, that sliver of light lit the tomb…

Is that not also our own experience of the dark night of the soul?

In one of my earlier books (*Last Chance,* Wood Lake Books, 1989), I suggested that Jesus' life and death were themselves an enacted parable, which went something like this:

> Once there was a sovereign who organized his realm to be totally just, totally fair to everyone. To test the system, he disguised himself as a poor person, one who had no position or status to protect him.
>
> As might be expected, he got into trouble, and was wrongly arrested. He was brought to trial. But he remained confident that he would ultimately receive justice. He had so much confidence in that ultimate justice that he refused to reveal his true identity. He didn't defend himself against false charges. Not even when he was beaten, not even when he was sentenced, not even when he was being executed, did he stop believing that in the end, justice would be done.

I concluded: "The parable remains unfinished; we have to supply the ending. If the parable ends on the cross, we would have to conclude that his confidence was misplaced. He did not receive the justice he expected. But if it ends not on Good Friday but on Easter morning, then he was blindingly, blazingly, right."

Ponderings
- How do insights come to you? By intuition or by reasoning? Slowly or quickly?
- What has been the happiest moment of your life? Did it surprise you?
- What was the darkest moment of your life? How did light come into it?

Prayer
Whenever I encounter an empty tomb in my life, keep me from crawling into it and pulling the stone shut behind me. Encourage me to leap joyously out of it into a new dawn.

John 20:19–23
All: Pentecost, A

Our modern Pentecost has settled down to a single Sunday of the year, based on Luke's timetable in Acts 2. But the early church may not have been as uniform. John offered Christian communities an alternate version of Pentecost, which happened the same day as Christ's resurrection.

As a writer, I can't help wondering why the writer of John's gospel deliberately develops a different chronology from Luke's.

As I've noted before, Luke's Gospel and Acts isolate the coming of the Holy Spirit from Jesus' resurrection by 50 days. But John makes the gift of the spirit almost immediate. "When it was evening, that day, the first day of the week... he breathed on them and said to them, 'Receive the Holy Spirit...'"

Why would John deliberately contradict Luke? Did he not know about Luke's version? Luke's gospel and Acts were both written some 20 years earlier. The early church clearly passed its writings around. I have as much difficulty believing that John knew nothing about Luke as I would have believing that Beethoven was never influenced by Bach or Mozart.

John's version of Pentecost differs from Luke's in that the Spirit does not arrive independently. Rather, Jesus confers the Spirit directly on his disciples. He breathes on them, and says specifically, "Receive the Holy Spirit."

All I can do, this many centuries later, is guess. John continually treats God and Jesus as an inseparable unity. He starts with that notion: "In the beginning was the Word, and the Word was with God, and the Word was God" (John 1:1). John has Jesus himself say, "The Father and I are one" (John 10:30). That unity is the central theme of chapters 14–17.

Perhaps John saw the unity of Father, Son, and Holy Spirit disintegrating into three disparate roles, prompted by Luke's 50-day separation. Instead of contradicting Luke, John tells a story that ties all three inseparably together.

When Jesus breathes on his disciples, he assumes God's role. In Genesis 2:7, God "breathed into his [Adam's] nostrils the breath of life; and the man became a living being." Breath and spirit are the same word, in both Hebrew (*ruach*) and Greek (*pneuma*). By breathing a new spirit into the clay of his disciples, the risen Jesus draws the three persons of the Trinity into One.

Ponderings
- When have you experienced new life?
- How significant is the festival of Pentecost in your worship life?
- Should churches always agree on everything?

Prayer
God, your spirit is everywhere. I should not expect it to be confined to a single story.

John 20:19-31
All: Easter 2, ABC

This reading includes the preceding one.

As a natural skeptic, I find it comforting that right from the beginning people have had trouble believing in the Resurrection. In modern times, Thomas would probably be an engineer. Engineers work with real things, with materials that can be handled and shaped and combined. In workshops I have led, almost without exception, if someone is struggling with symbolism or metaphor, it's an engineer. (I say that without disrespect, for I almost became an engineer myself.)

Thomas *wants* to believe. Just as he'd like to believe that a city has a spirit, that it is more than streets and buildings. Or that a car could have feelings. Or that a book can shine with holiness. But he'll have to be shown.

This reading is, in one sense, the resurrection of Thomas.

The others saw the tomb, heard the word, and believed. Thomas needed to know for himself.

Our churches are filled with people who believe, because they know someone else who believes, who knows someone else… The chain can go a long way back, and the first-hand experience of God gets a bit more diluted each time.

That's why Thomas's story belongs here. We usually tell it as a story about doubt, casting guilt upon those who may similarly harbor hesitations about religious dogma. If good old Thomas can conquer his doubts and believe, if he can say "My Lord and my God," so should we.

It might better be portrayed as a story about a person who has new life breathed into old bones. This is Ezekiel's parable of the "valley of the dry bones" (Ezekiel 37:1-14) turned into a personal experience. If Jesus was the Word made flesh, this is scripture made flesh.

For a writer, this chapter feels like the original end of John's gospel. John wraps the story up. Jesus has breathed his spirit into the disciples, putting his life into them as God put life into the clay figures in the Garden of Eden. The skeptical believe, and others will believe them. And the final verse sums up the entire gospel: "Jesus did many other signs…but these are written so that you may believe…"

Ponderings
- Can doubt be healthy? How?
- What kind of evidence do you require to convince you?
- Have you had any experiences that caused you to express something like, "My Lord and my God!"?

Prayer
I want to believe. I do. Please, God, Jesus, or whoever you are, help my unbelief.

John 21:1-19
All: Easter 3, C

The epilogue to John's gospel describes the disciples' final encounter with Jesus, on the shores of the Lake of Galilee. Like all epilogues, this one has been tacked on after the ending. But why? Several things happen.
- It returns the gospel story to Galilee, where it began.
- It reprises the original calling of the disciples from their boats.
- It gives Peter three chances to undo his three denials in the high priest's courtyard.

Perhaps, when the first readers finished chapter 20, they protested that John – in his haste to get to the giving of the Holy Spirit, the reason for the church's existence – had left Peter in disgrace. He was a coward. He had denied his relationship with his leader. He was a failure. He had missed the point of Jesus' last teachings about love by resorting to violence. How could such a man have become the leader of their church?

So John tells a story that puts Peter back in God's good books.

I'm intrigued at the different emphases that people pull from this passage. Several focus on verse 18, in which Jesus apparently predicts that Peter too would be imprisoned and executed. One colleague saw it as a universal truth about growing old, about losing control over one's life. Eventually, he suggested, we are all as helpless as Peter or Paul being led to their executions.

To my skeptical editor's eye, verse 18 reads like an insert, jammed into the manuscript after the fact. As I've noted before, John writes natural dialogue. And this comment comes right out of the blue. It has no natural connection to the conversation about sheep. It's not characteristic of John.

What is characteristic of John, to my mind, is the metaphorical give and take of verses 15-17. As in other incidents, John gives both sides of the dialogue. You can hear it, say it, feel it. John even identifies the emotions Peter felt.

Sheep don't eat fish, of course. But then, neither do they eat shavings. Yet in John 10, the carpenter from Nazareth describes himself as the Good Shepherd. Like his claim to be the light and the bread, it was a figurative use of language.

So these verses can't be read literally either.

As I read the multiple levels of meaning in these lines, I hear Jesus saying, "Peter, I'm leaving you. I can't be the 'Good Shepherd' for all those sheep anymore. You're going to have to take over as their 'Good Shepherd' in my place."

For a short time, people had been able to see in Jesus as much as they could comprehend of God. When Jesus left, they would have to see Jesus in Peter.

Like David, Peter had to be anointed twice. The first time (in Matthew 16:17-19 and parallels) Peter was as unready as the boy David for his future responsibilities. But eventually David was ready. And so, eventually, was Peter.

That's the reason for adding the epilogue. It's John's version of the Great Commissioning (Matthew 28:18-20).

Ponderings

- Would you like to have a second chance to undo mistakes you've made?
- When things go wrong, do you retreat into familiar situations where you feel more confident?
- Who are Jesus' sheep? What does it mean to feed them?

Prayer

I've come this far with you, Jesus. Now I have to continue on my own. God help me.

John 21:20-25
ELC: St. John, ABC

Several stylistic clues indicate to me that this chapter was tacked on by the early church. First, there's that nice ending to the previous chapter. Then there's that conversation with Peter that fails to ring true. Finally, there's this discussion about John's death. The careful wording suggests to me that John had, in fact, died before his gospel went into circulation – and some doubters believed that his failure to keep living in some way invalidated his witness.

Verse 24 concludes, significantly, with the only reference in the entire gospel to "we know that his testimony is true." It's like an editor's footnote. Nowhere else does any "we" attempt to authenticate the disciple's own "testimony."

The epilogue ends with a warning. Perhaps even by the time John's gospel was written, Christians had started to put the written records of the new church onto a pedestal. Like some branches of today's church, they had begun to treat the text itself as sacred.

In his life, Jesus had criticized those who made the Hebrew scriptures a straitjacket. Now his own followers were doing the same. The encounters with God were sacred; the story of those encounters was not.

So the editors who circulated John's gospel added a final caution – the risen Christ can never be confined to the pages of this book, or any book.

Ponderings
- When did God's revelation to us come to an end?
- Do you treat the Bible differently from other books?
- Do you ever add a PS to your letters?

Prayer
Jesus, you told Peter not to fuss over the details, but just to follow you. Keep me too from fussing over details instead of following you.

LEADING A STUDY GROUP

You don't have to be the expert to lead a group. Ideally, you should know a little more than the members of the group – and usually, simply by checking some reference materials in preparation for each session, you will.

But in fact, even if you don't know more than some members of the group, you can still perform your primary function – to facilitate free and open discussion.

The only real authority in any Bible study group is the biblical text itself. Participants may wonder what the text means. They may question its accuracy or validity. They may reword it for clarity. They may even reject its message. But they have to work with what's there.

Code of conduct

Free and open discussion does not come about naturally. Some people dominate discussion, others hold back. Some people tend to be opinionated; others prefer being malleable.

To improve the likelihood of free and open discussion, start your group off on the right foot. Draw up a code of conduct, a set of expectations. Hand it out at the beginning, and ask members to agree to it.

If one or two members later create dissension, you can remind them of what they agreed to.

A code of conduct might include the following points:

1. We are all adults, and responsible for our own learning. We will treat each other with respect.
2. Each person's experience is equally valid.
3. We may ask questions about another person's experience or beliefs, but we may not dispute those experiences and beliefs.
4. Each person is entitled to his or her own opinion.
5. There are no stupid questions, and no wrong answers.
6. Each of us is here to grow in our faith, whatever it may be at this moment. We will not attempt to argue another person into a particular point of view.

7. Every person will have the opportunity to express his or her views, or to remain silent.

These sound relatively innocuous, but they will prevent arrogant persons from humiliating or browbeating others later. And they will keep both biblical literalists and militant agnostics from imposing their personal perspectives on others.

Commentaries and reference materials

Encourage participants to read and bring to each session their own reference materials.

These should include at least one contemporary translation of the Bible. Those who have a deep attachment to the rich language of older translations such as the King James Version may use them, of course, but they will find much less difficulty understanding passages if they also have available a current translation.

Some Bibles – sometimes called "Scholar's" or "Study" versions – include their own commentaries. All commentaries have a bias. They may be liberal or conservative; they may lean to the right or the left; they may take a literal or a critical perspective. It doesn't matter – as long as no member of the group is allowed to argue that *this* commentary has the *only* acceptable approach.

Encourage members to consult and use *any* commentary. The diversity of views will stimulate consideration of concepts that members may not have thought about before.

Provide a friendly environment

How you set up the meeting room will significantly affect the quality of discussion and the learning that results from it.

Unless you have invited a professor to give a lecture, don't set up rows of chairs like a classroom!

If you're meeting in a church, set chairs around a table. The table allows participants to sit relatively close to each other without feeling crowded. They also have a place to put their Bibles and commentaries.

If you're meeting in a more informal setting, such as someone's home, arrange seating in a circle. Provide as many comfortable chairs as possible. Depending on the age of the participants, cushions on the floor may also work.

I try to restrict the length of sessions to two hours maximum – although sometimes the members take control and keep going longer. A one-hour session is often too short; members are just getting warmed up when the session is cut off.

A break, halfway through, allows shy people to express their thoughts in private, and often opens up much richer discussion afterwards.

Refreshments help to create a relaxed environment – whether at the beginning, at a midway break, or at the end of the session. If nothing else, make tea, coffee, and juice available. Better yet, invite participants to take turns bringing cookies, crackers, cheese, fruit, or almost any form of snack. Sharing food together is not only a long-honored Christian tradition, it makes good sense too!

The purpose of the gathering

Bible study has only one purpose. The members are there to grow in their faith. They can only grow as they connect new information (which includes personal stories) to the structure of beliefs that they already have. The new information may challenge their faith, or it may reinforce it. But it has to connect.

Lectures can provide information. But it takes a very skilled lecturer to evoke connections between the text of the Bible and the audience's personal experiences.

On the other hand, when people talk about their own life experiences in the context of Bible study, they cannot help making connections for themselves. By talking about what they hear in the text, by sharing their doubts and their insights, they associate their new learning with what they already know, and lock it into place.

Bible study may open up conversations that could not, and would not, happen otherwise. "I've worked beside that man for 30 years," said a participant in one program, "and I've never heard him talk about those things before." Studying a biblical text invites people to dig into their deepest convictions and values.

But a word of warning – a Bible study session is not a therapy group. If the discussion starts repeatedly focusing on one person's problems, it's time to intervene. Neither you as leader, nor members of the group, should attempt to act as counselor. Sometimes, the person merely needs to realize that he or she is monopolizing the group. Other times, he or she may need referral to a professional counselor. Resolving such a situation will depend on tact and sensitivity. But don't let one person's concerns destroy the possibilities for everyone else.

Your role as leader

Your primary role is to guide the discussion. The best way to do that is by asking questions.

In studying the Bible, I find the best process is usually the simplest. Invite some member of the group to read aloud a paragraph from the book being studied. Reading aloud does three things. It enables members to hear nuances that they might not notice otherwise. It establishes a model of speaking out loud, rather than thinking to oneself. And it makes the learning a collective experience rather than a private one.

Encourage members to interrupt at anything that strikes them: a startling variation in wording between versions of the Bible, for example, or an unexpected implication in a statement. However, few people have the confidence (or brashness) to interrupt when someone else is reading what they may think of as a sacred book.

Invite questions or comments when the paragraph ends. It's preferable if the focus of discussion arises from the group itself, rather than being imposed by a leader. However, if nothing emerges, you will have to ask questions to stimulate discussion.

In general, ask the kind of questions that encourage participants to tell stories. Their convictions and beliefs do not exist in isolation. They result from their life experiences. Seemingly strange beliefs can turn out to make a lot of sense, given that person's experiences.

So ask open-ended questions – that is, questions that can't be answered with a simple yes or no, or with just a few words. Ask about feelings, impressions, concerns. Don't ask the kind that might appear on an examination paper, to see who's been paying attention. (One technique for cutting off a long-winded narration is to interrupt with a closed question, one that requires a precise answer.

Having thus reasserted control, you can immediately re-direct the discussion to some other participant.)

And ask follow-up questions. Unless an answer has already gone on too long, show interest by picking up on some aspect of the person's comments and probe a little deeper. Most people are flattered that someone has actually listened to them and wants to hear more.

"Why?" is always a good follow-up question. Or, "What led you to that opinion?" "When did you first start feeling that way?"

But don't keep coming back to the same person with a series of follow-up questions. After one follow-up, or at most two, move on to someone else. Do they agree, or disagree? Why?

As a former moderator of the United Church of Canada once observed, it is almost impossible to ask "Why?" more than three or four times without getting into questions of ultimate purpose and meaning – that is, into theology.

Permit silence, too. As leader, you don't have to rush in just because people are not speaking for a moment. They may need the silence as a time to think. Better yet, someone else in the group may volunteer his or her own questions or responses.

You can, if you wish, use the "Ponderings" questions associated with the readings in this commentary to stimulate thought. Or you can use the following four questions as the basis for discussing almost any scriptural passage. Don't use the questions as a formula, though. Rephrase the questions into your own words, and modify them to match the discussion already taking place.

1. What was actually happening here, in your own words?
2. What made it important to the people taking part?
3. Why would someone want to write this down, so that future generations could read it?
4. Why do you think it's significant for us, in our time?

LECTIONARY INDEX

Reading	Sunday, RCL	Year
Jn 01:(1-9) 10-18	Christmas	ABC
Jn 01:1-14	Christmas	ABC
Jn 01:1-18		ABC
Jn 01:1-18		ABC
Jn 01:1-5, 9-14		B
Jn 01:6-8, 19-28	Advent 3	B
Jn 01:29-42	Epiphany 2	A
Jn 01:35-42		ABC
Jn 01:35-42		B
Jn 01:43-51	Epiphany 2	B
Jn 01:43-51		ABC
Jn 02:1-11	Epiphany 2	C
Jn 02:13-22		ABC
Jn 02:13-22	Lent 3	B
Jn 03:1-17	Lent 2 (alternate)	A
Jn 03:1-17	Trinity	B
Jn 03:13-17	Holy Cross (Sep 14)	ABC
Jn 03:13-17		ABC
Jn 03:14-21	Lent 4	B
Jn 03:16-18		A
Jn 04:5-42	Lent 3	A
Jn 05:1-9	Easter 6 (alternate)	C
Jn 06:1-21	Proper 12 [17] (Jul 24-30)	B
Jn 06:24-35	Proper 13 [18] (Jul 31-Aug 6)	B
Jn 06:25-35	Thanksgiving	C
Jn 06:35, 41-51	Proper 14 [19] (Aug 7-13)	B
Jn 06:51-58	Proper 15 [20] (Aug 14-20)	B
Jn 06:51-59		A
Jn 06:56-69	Proper 16 [21] (Aug 21-27)	B
Jn 07:37-39	Pentecost (alternate)	A
Jn 08:1-11		C

Sunday, RC	Sunday, ELC
	Christmas 2
	Christmas
Christmas	
Christmas 2	Christmas 2
All Souls	
Advent 3	Advent 3
Ordinary 2	Epiphany 2
	St. Andrew (Nov 30)
Ordinary 2	
	Epiphany 2
	St. Bartholomew (Aug 24)
Ordinary 2	Epiphany 2
St. John Lateran	
Lent 3	Lent 3
	Lent 2
	Trinity
	Holy Cross
Triumph of the Cross	
Lent 4	Lent 4
Holy Trinity	
Lent 3	Lent 3
	Easter 6 (alternate)
Ordinary 17	Proper 12
Ordinary 18	Proper 13
	Thanksgiving
Ordinary 19	Proper 14
Ordinary 20	Proper 15
Corpus Christi (Thursday after Trinity)	
Ordinary 21	Proper 16
Pentecost Vigil	Pentecost Vigil
Lent 5	

LECTIONARY INDEX

Reading	Sunday, RCL	Year
Jn 08:31-36		ABC
Jn 09:1-41	Lent 4	A
Jn 10:1-10	Easter 4	A
Jn 10:11-18	Easter 4	B
Jn 10:22-30	Easter 4	C
Jn 11:1-45	Lent 5	A
Jn 11:32-44	All Saints	B
Jn 12:1-8	Lent 5	C
Jn 12:1-11	Monday of Holy Week	ABC
Jn 12:12-16	Palm Sunday	B
Jn 12:20-33	Lent 5	B
Jn 12:20-36	Tuesday in Holy Week	ABC
Jn 12:23-26		A
Jn 13:1-17, 31b-35	Thursday in Holy Week	ABC
Jn 13:21-32	Wednesday in Holy Week	ABC
Jn 13:31-35	Easter 5	C
Jn 14:1-14	Easter 5	A
Jn 14:1-17		ABC
Jn 14:8-14		ABC
Jn 14:8-17 (25-27)	Pentecost	C
Jn 14:15-21	Easter 6	A
Jn 14:21-27		ABC
Jn 14:23-29	Easter 6 (alternate)	C
Jn 15:1-8	Easter 5	B
Jn 15:9-17	Easter 6	B
Jn 15:26-27, 16:4b-15	Pentecost	B
Jn 16:12-15	Trinity	C
Jn 17:1-11	Easter 7	A
Jn 17:6-19	Easter 7	B
Jn 17:11-19		B

Sunday, RC	Sunday, ELC
	Reformation Day (Oct 31)
Lent 4	Lent 4
Easter 4	Easter 4
Easter 4	Easter 4
Easter 4	Easter 4
Lent 5	Lent 5
	Lent 5
	Monday of Holy Week
Palm Sunday	
Lent 5	Lent 5
	Tuesday of Holy Week
All Souls	
Thursday of Holy Week	Thursday of Holy Week
	Wednesday of Holy Week
Easter 5	Easter 5
Easter 5	Easter 5
	St. Thomas (Dec. 21)
	St. Philip & St. James (May 1)
Pentecost	Pentecost
Easter 6	Easter 6
	St. Simon & St. Jude (Oct 28)
Easter 6	Easter 6 (alternate)
Easter 5	Easter 5
Easter 6	Easter 6
Pentecost	Pentecost
Holy Trinity	Trinity
Easter 7	Easter 7
Easter 7	Easter 7
Easter 7 (US)	

LECTIONARY INDEX

Reading	Sunday, RCL	Year
Jn 17:20-26	Easter 7	C
Jn 18:1 - 19:42	Good Friday	ABC
Jn 18:33-37	Reign of Christ (Nov 20-26)	B
Jn 19:31-37		B
Jn 19:38-42	Saturday of Holy Week	ABC
Jn 20:1-2, 11-18		ABC
Jn 20:1-9		ABC
Jn 20:1-18	Easter	ABC
Jn 20:11-18		C
Jn 20:19-23	Pentecost	A
Jn 20:19-31	Easter 2	ABC
Jn 21:1-19	Easter 3	C
Jn 21:20-25		ABC

Sunday, RC	Sunday, ELC
Easter 7	Easter 7
Good Friday (Passion of Our Lord)	Good Friday
Christ the King	Christ the King
Sacred Heart	
	St. Mary Magdalene (Jul 22)
Easter (US)	
Easter	Easter
All Souls	
Pentecost	Pentecost (alternate)
Easter 2	Easter 2
Easter 3	Easter 3
	St. John (Dec 27)

SUNDAY INDEX

Sunday, RCL	Year	Sunday, RC
Advent 3	B	Advent 3
Christmas	ABC	
	ABC	Christmas
Christmas 2	ABC	
	ABC	Christmas 2
Epiphany 2	A	Ordinary 2
Epiphany 2	C	Ordinary 2
Epiphany 2	B	
	B	Ordinary 2
Lent 2 (alternate)	A	
Lent 3	A	Lent 3
Lent 3	B	Lent 3
Lent 4	A	Lent 4
Lent 4	B	Lent 4
Lent 5	A	Lent 5
Lent 5	B	Lent 5
Lent 5	C	
	C	Lent 5
Palm Sunday	B	Palm Sunday
Monday of Holy Week	ABC	
Tuesday in Holy Week	ABC	
Wednesday in Holy Week	ABC	
Thursday in Holy Week	ABC	Thursday of Holy Week
Good Friday	ABC	Good Friday
Saturday of Holy Week	ABC	

Sunday, ELC	Reading
Advent 3	Jn 01:6-8, 19-28
Christmas	Jn 01:1-14
	Jn 01:1-18
Christmas 2	Jn 01:(1-9) 10-18
	Jn 01:1-18
Epiphany 2	Jn 01:29-42
Epiphany 2	Jn 02:1-11
Epiphany 2	Jn 01:43-51
	Jn 01:35-42
Lent 2	Jn 03:1-17
Lent 3	Jn 04:5-42
Lent 3	Jn 02:13-22
Lent 4	Jn 09:1-41
Lent 4	Jn 03:14-21
Lent 5	Jn 11:1-45
Lent 5	Jn 12:20-33
Lent 5	Jn 12:1-8
	Jn 08:1-11
	Jn 12:12-16
Monday of Holy Week	Jn 12:1-11
Tuesday of Holy Week	Jn 12:20-36
Wednesday of Holy Week	Jn 13:21-32
Thursday of Holy Week	Jn 13:1-17, 31b-35
Good Friday	Jn 18:1 - 19:42
	Jn 19:38-42

SUNDAY INDEX

Sunday, RCL	Year	Sunday, RC
Easter	ABC	Easter
	ABC	Easter (US)
Easter 2	ABC	Easter 2
Easter 3	C	Easter 3
Easter 4	A	Easter 4
Easter 4	B	Easter 4
Easter 4	C	Easter 4
Easter 5	A	Easter 5
Easter 5	B	Easter 5
Easter 5	C	Easter 5
Easter 6	A	Easter 6
Easter 6	B	Easter 6
Easter 6 (alternate)	C	Easter 6
Easter 6 (alternate)	C	
Easter 7	A	Easter 7
Easter 7	B	Easter 7
Easter 7	C	Easter 7
	B	Easter 7 (US)
Pentecost	B	Pentecost
Pentecost	C	Pentecost
Pentecost	A	Pentecost
Pentecost (alternate)	A	Pentecost Vigil
	A	Holy Trinity
Trinity	C	Holy Trinity
Trinity	B	
	A	Corpus Christi (Thu

Sunday, ELC	Reading
Easter	Jn 20:1-18
	Jn 20:1-9
Easter 2	Jn 20:19-31
Easter 3	Jn 21:1-19
Easter 4	Jn 10:1-10
Easter 4	Jn 10:11-18
Easter 4	Jn 10:22-30
Easter 5	Jn 14:1-14
Easter 5	Jn 15:1-8
Easter 5	Jn 13:31-35
Easter 6	Jn 14:15-21
Easter 6	Jn 15:9-17
Easter 6 (alternate)	Jn 14:23-29
Easter 6 (alternate)	Jn 05:1-9
Easter 7	Jn 17:1-11
Easter 7	Jn 17:6-19
Easter 7	Jn 17:20-26
	Jn 17:11-19
Pentecost	Jn 15:26-27, 16:4b-15
Pentecost	Jn 14:8-17 (25-27)
Pentecost (alternate)	Jn 20:19-23
Pentecost Vigil	Jn 07:37-39
	Jn 03:16-18
Trinity	Jn 16:12-15
Trinity	Jn 03:1-17
(Trinity)	Jn 06:51-59

SUNDAY INDEX

Sunday, RCL	Year	Sunday, RC
Proper 12 [17] (Jul 24-30)	B	Ordinary 17
Proper 13 [18] (Jul 31-Aug 6)	B	Ordinary 18
Proper 14 [19] (Aug 7-13)	B	Ordinary 19
Proper 15 [20] (Aug 14-20)	B	Ordinary 20
Proper 16 [21] (Aug 21-27)	B	Ordinary 21
Holy Cross (Sep 14)	ABC	
Thanksgiving	C	
All Saints	B	
	A	All Souls
	B	All Souls
	C	All Souls
Reign of Christ (Nov 20-26)	B	Christ the King

Sunday, ELC	Reading
Proper 12	Jn 06:1-21
Proper 13	Jn 06:24-35
Proper 14	Jn 06:35, 41-51
Proper 15	Jn 06:51-58
Proper 16	Jn 06:56-69
Holy Cross	Jn 03:13-17
Thanksgiving	Jn 06:25-35
	Jn 11:32-44
	Jn 12:23-26
	Jn 01:1-5, 9-14
	Jn 20:11-18
Christ the King	Jn 18:33-37

Other titles by Wood Lake Books for Group Study

The Spirit of Life
Five Studies to Bring Us Closer to the Heart of God
IAN PRICE
Guides readers through a five-session group study of selected scripture passages to explore themes such as Goodness, Order, Mercy, Power, and Wholeness.
ISBN 1-55145-432-7

A Sensual Faith
Experiencing God Through Our Senses
IAN PRICE
This five-session group study explores each of the five senses as a doorway to deepening our faith and encountering God.
ISBN 1-55145-502-1

Jacob's Blessing
Dreams, Hopes and Visions for the Church
DONNA SINCLAIR & CHRISTOPHER WHITE
A hopeful and inspirational vision of the future of the church. Video and study guide also available.
ISBN Book: 1-55145-381-9
ISBN Video: 1-55145-388-6

Dying Church Living God
A Call to Begin Again
CHUCK MEYER
Challenges those in the pews and outside the tent to renew the church.
ISBN 1-896836-39-9

Find these titles at any fine bookstore, or call 1.800.663.2775 for more information. Check our website www.joinhands.com

More titles from Northstone Publishing that stimulate discussion

Religious Abuse
A Pastor Explores the Many Ways Religion Can Hurt As Well As Heal
KEITH WRIGHT
This positive book opens the door to discussion of an issue that affects millions of churchgoers.
ISBN 1-896836-47-X

Prayer: *The Hidden Fire*
TOM HARPUR
Brings the broad theological perspective of prayer to the personal level.
ISBN 1-896836-40-2

Spiritscapes
Mapping the Spiritual and Scientific Terrain at the Dawn of the New Millennium
MARK PARENT
An overview and analysis of nine of the most significant spiritual and scientific movements of our time.
ISBN 1-896836-11-9

Secret Affairs of the Soul
Ordinary People's Extraordinary Experiences of the Sacred
PAUL HAWKER
Firsthand accounts of spiritual experiences from a broad range of individuals.
ISBN 1-896836-42-9

Northstone is an imprint of Wood Lake Books Inc.

Find these titles at any fine bookstore, or call 1.800.663.2775 for more information. Check our website www.joinhands.com

Other books by James Taylor you might enjoy…

Precious Days and Practical Love
Caring for Your Aging Parent
Practical advice on the changing relationship with aging parents.
ISBN 1-896836-34-8

SIN: *A New Understanding of Virtue and Vice*
Examines the fascinating origins and evolution of all seven deadly sins.
ISBN 1-896836-00-3

Letters to Stephen
A Father's Journey of Grief and Recovery
For those who have survived a death – be it of a person, a relationship, a career, or a concept – personal letters and thought-provoking discussions about grief.
ISBN 1-55145-054-2

Everyday Psalms
The Psalms live again in images and language from contemporary experience.
ISBN 1-55145-045-3

Everyday Parables
Rediscovering God in common things.
ISBN 1-55145-055-0

You'll also find Jim Taylor's writing on the Internet through www.joinhands.com. Click on "Jim's site" for *Edges*: reflections linking faith and everyday life.

Sharp Edges: a more trenchant political and social commentary, updated weekly. .

Find these titles at any fine bookstore, or call 1.800.663.2775 for more information. Check our website www.joinhands.com